So You Want to be a Dog Trainer

Step-by-Step Advice from a Professional

Nicole Wilde

So You Want To Be A Dog Trainer
by Nicole Wilde

Copyright © 2001 by Nicole Wilde

Published by:
Phantom Publishing
P.O. Box 2814
Santa Clarita, CA 91386

First Edition

ISBN 0-9667726-2-8

Back cover photo: Tia Torres
All other photos by the author.

For Mojo, Soko,
Phantom, Heyoka and Sequoia

Other books by the author:

Living with Wolfdogs

Wolfdogs A-Z: Behavior, Training & More

ACKNOWLEDGEMENTS

I would like to thank the following:

Dr. Ian Dunbar for his support, friendship and encouragement. Without Ian I never would have published the first book, never mind the next two.

Laura Bourhenne for her generosity, feedback and uncanny ability to catch those errors no one else does. And thanks to her Mom, Dorothy Williams, the Grammar Queen.

Mychelle and Jake Blake for allowing me to use their lovely dogs as head halter/collar models.

Thanks as always to my wonderful husband C.C., who not only reads each manuscript, but provides encouragement, support and puts up with me when things aren't going well. I really did marry the best guy in the world.

Last but never least, I would like to thank Mojo, Soko, Phantom, Heyoka, Sequioa and the countless dogs and wolves who have given me love, laughter and lessons over the years. They will always be my best and most beloved teachers.

Table of Contents

Group Classes

Endnote

Resources

Introduction

No doubt you've noticed there are countless books and videos on the market about how to train your dog. Most are geared toward the average pet owner, and focus on training techniques and resolving common behavior problems. But what if your goal is not simply to train your own dog, but to become a professional trainer? Where do you turn for information on running your business, advertising, dealing with clients and teaching classes? There certainly doesn't seem to be a glut of books out there. Of course, what would be really helpful would be to have a friend in the business, someone who has been a professional dog trainer for years and is willing to give you the inside scoop; someone who would let you in on trade secrets, offer motivation and share great ideas. Think of me as that friend.

We'll take it step by step. First, we'll discuss factors that will help you to decide whether a dog training career is truly something you want to pursue. Then we'll talk about what type of training you might do, how to go about getting an education (which, by the way, doesn't necessarily mean going back to school), the nuts and bolts of setting up your business, tips on dealing with clients and much more. All this, and you don't even have to buy me dinner.

Sit back and relax. Let me tell you a story... When I was fourteen, my Mom registered me and my Schipperke mix, Skippy (don't blame me, Dad named the dog) for a group obedience class. I was excited beyond belief. Becoming a dog trainer was one of those secret dreams I harbored but would never admit to my parents. In my family, you were expected to finish school and get the sort of job you could "fall back on," something stable and secure; at any rate, nothing so frivolous as dog training. I couldn't wait for the big day to arrive.

The first class was filled with anxious dogs and nervous owners. We listened carefully as the instructor explained each exercise, then demonstrated it with a student's dog. Although I was surprised that so much pushing and pulling was involved, I dutifully tried each one with Skippy. It soon became clear that although she was extremely intelligent, Skippy was not having fun. I was no expert, but she seemed pretty uncomfortable. The instructor, who was actually a very nice woman, honestly believed that a lot of force was necessary to get the dogs to behave properly. The dogs were jerked roughly by a choke chain if they didn't "obey" and when they did obey, it was out of fear of punishment. Naturally, some of the dogs (and people) were quite stressed and therefore unable to learn. It became a vicious cycle of stress and corrections. I was horrified. I had no idea that dog training was so brutal! Though we completed the course, I was crushed. It was obvious I just didn't have what it took to be a dog trainer.

Now for the good news... fast forward twenty years. Dog training has changed for the better! Thanks to pioneers like Dr. Ian Dunbar, Karen Pryor, Jean Donaldson and others, more and more trainers are discovering the power and joy of positive training. Unlike traditional punishment-based methods, positive training uses rewards. Dogs are set up to succeed by making it easy for them to learn, and are then rewarded for performing correctly. Here's a training tip: *When a dog gets rewarded for something, he is likely to do that thing again.* It's simple! Best of all, reward-based training is not only effective, it is enjoyable for both dog and owner. Dog training actually can be fun!

I first got involved in training dogs through volunteering with an organization that rescues wolves and wolfdogs (wolf-dog mixes). In addition to the daily care, socialization and training of these animals, I went out on many calls to see wolfdog owners. I helped them with training, behavior issues, building enclosures, and whatever else would allow them to keep their animals. I never thought to charge for my services. Over the next ten years, while holding various office jobs, I wrote two books about wolfdogs, co-ran the rescue center for a few years, and began training dogs for the general public (for a fee). I found that while training wolves can be difficult, training domestic dogs is much easier; it's training people that can be challenging! I finally made the leap to training full-time as my own, one-person company. I now work with a variety of wonderful dogs on a daily basis, meet interesting people, set my own hours and enjoy a healthy income. Helping to modify the behavior of dogs who might otherwise be given up, assisting dogs in overcoming their fear/aggression issues, and in general, *helping dogs*—well, it's still pretty closely related to rescue if you think about it. To me, it is incredibly fulfilling. And to think, you actually get paid for this!

You may be thinking this all sounds wonderful, but there is some personal roadblock to your becoming a trainer. Perhaps you lack experience with dogs; maybe you believe you are too old to start a new career; or, you are afraid you are just not the type to give advice in an authoritative manner. Whatever your concern, put it aside for now. If you decide to become a dog trainer, and work hard for it, nothing will stop you. In fact, not only will we cover step-by-step how to start out and what to do each step along the way, we'll even go over strategies for overcoming a lack of confidence so you can make that leap to becoming a full-fledged, positively successful dog trainer. *So let's go!*

Why Do You Want to Train Dogs?

I've loved dogs since I was a kid. Maybe you have too, and that's why you want to be a dog trainer. In fact, that's the reason a lot of people get into this business, but it's not the only one. Some trainers like dogs well enough, but their real motivation is that dog training is a client-oriented service that allows them to work closely with people. There is a lot of person-to-person interaction in dog training, from coaxing information from clients, to patiently instructing them, giving support and encouragement. Some of the best trainers sincerely enjoy working with both dogs and humans. A third incentive for getting into dog training is financial gain. Let's examine each of these motivations.

"I Love Dogs!"

So you love dogs and want a career where you can work with them in a positive way. Maybe you enjoy the process of teaching dogs new skills. Perhaps you like puzzles and detective work, and think you might enjoy that aspect of solving behavior issues. Or, you'd simply like to help change dogs' behaviors so that they don't lose their homes. Great! This career just might be for you. You can do a world of good for dogs in the capacity of a professional trainer. For the dog lover, training can be extremely fulfilling on an emotional level. It is wonderful to see a dog who was formerly kept outdoors, now indoors and part of the family because he's now better behaved, thanks to your efforts. I can't begin to describe the joy I feel when a client says, "We were so close to giving this dog up. Thank you for helping us to be able to keep him. We really love him." How's *that* for job satisfaction? It is a real thrill too, to get to the heart of a behavior issue, design a program to address it, then watch progress being made. Seeing

1

a dog who was frightened of people accept petting and treats from strangers is heart-warming. Watching a dog who was reactive toward others dogs romp and play with them is amazing. And seeing the joy and love that exists between a dog and its family, knowing they can now stay together, is priceless.

While having a love of and compassion for canines is conducive to being a great trainer, it can also make your job difficult at times. You will inevitably visit homes where the dog is kept in poor conditions, ignored or even abused. If you deal with aggressive dogs, there will be cases where the owner, perhaps with your input, makes the decision to euthanize. Will these cases cause you to lose sleep, or to become depressed or angry? Those reactions would certainly be understandable. But think carefully, and be honest with yourself. Would those issues cause you only temporary distress or would they, over time, wear on your emotional well-being? There is a lot of responsibility involved in helping an owner to make a life and death decision, and there surely will be cases where, despite your best efforts, the situation is just not salvageable. Would you blame yourself if that happened, or know that you did your best under the circumstances? On a less dramatic note, will you be able to assess situations objectively and give constructive advice, rather than blurt out things like, "Of course he's destroying things, he's chained up and bored to tears!" Trust me, there are times we all want to shout the latter, and doing the former takes self-control—but it's necessary. You owe it to yourself to think realistically about whether you can deal with the emotional issues that come up in dog training. For the most part, though, there are vastly more positive outcomes than negative, and much that is emotionally rewarding.

"I'm a People Person"

Many people get into dog training because they enjoy working with and helping people. Consider this very carefully, because *at least half of dog training is really training the owners.* This is a customer service business. You will deal with all types of people. Some will be absolutely wonderful, some ignorant, and a few, downright unpleasant. You absolutely need "people skills" as well as canine skills to be a good, effective trainer. Having a background in psychology or social work helps but is not necessary. Having empathy for people and treating them kindly and with patience, is. No one wants to hear that they're doing it all wrong, no matter how badly they're doing it. You must develop a talent for finding the good and praising it in people, just as you do with dogs. When a client just doesn't get what you're trying to show them and fumbles it over and over, what will you do? Will you see it as a training problem, and patiently break the task into smaller, more manageable steps? Or will you get frustrated and lose your cool?

You will find yourself in homes with screaming, out-of-control children (my toughest personal challenge), and clients who take phone calls in the middle of your session. Some will argue with everything you say, while others will argue with their spouses or children in front of you. I have found myself in situations where I'd swear I was watching the television show *Family Feud.* It was all I could do not to shout out, "Good answer! Good answer!" Take a deep breath and ask yourself whether this type of scenario is something you realistically can, or want to, deal with. Keep in mind that I'm laying out the worst cases here so you can really consider everything. The fact is, most people you'll work with are friendly and want what's best for their dog. After all, that's why they called a trainer in the first place. Most are willing to listen and will appreciate your assistance. Many will tell you how much the training has helped. It doesn't hurt your ego, either, when you get a dog to behave differently and the client, amazed, asks when you can move in with them. (Nothing wrong with a little positive reinforcement for the trainer!) I have met so many wonderful people over the years who I never would have had the opportunity to meet otherwise. I have become friends with some and have stayed in touch with others just because they and their dogs were so pleasant to deal with. If you enjoy meeting a variety of people and can be patient while teaching them, this career may be for you.

Ka-Ching!

Now we come to the part that you may be unsure about—finances. Can you really make a decent living as a dog trainer? Yes, and even better than decent. Will you make a fortune? Probably not, especially at the beginning. Like any other business, it's tough when you start out. With most businesses, it takes an average of a year for word of mouth to start getting around. Dog training is no exception. Another business maxim is that it usually takes about three years to turn a profit. In dog training, unless you have overhead to pay on a training center, you should be able to get things rolling in a much shorter amount of time. Of course, you will still incur expenses such as insurance, training equipment, advertising and so forth, but if you market yourself well, do a good job and people like you, you can begin to turn a profit relatively quickly.

A safe way to ease into dog training is to work at a full-time or part-time job while training on the side. As your business builds, you can gradually switch over to training full time. Some people opt to train part-time on a permanent basis. That's one of the great things about this career. You get to make your own hours, and eventually, to dictate how much or how little you work.

What type of training you choose to do will largely determine your income. Group classes have been called the "bread and butter" of the dog trainer's business. It is true that group classes afford a more steady income than the hit-and-miss scheduling of private, one-on-one appointments. Clients normally sign up for an average of eight group lessons in advance, which ensures a guaranteed weekly income over that period. Some trainers do nothing but group classes, love what they do, and earn a great living at it. In the next chapter we will discuss different types of group classes you could offer.

Some trainers earn a substantial income doing only private, in-home training. This can include obedience work, but more often focuses on behavior issues. Once word of mouth gets around and your business becomes established, you could end up doing anywhere from five to twenty in-home appointments a week. The down side of in-home appointments is the last-minute cancellations and lack of steady scheduling during slow times such as holidays and vacation periods.

An option you might not have considered is board-and-train. This means that you keep the client's dog at your own home (or kennel, if you're lucky enough to have one) and train it there for an agreed upon length of time. Board-and-train can be quite profitable, and gives you valuable one-on-one time with the dog. (More on board-and-train in the next section.) Some trainers not only do board-and-train, but offer plain old boarding as well. If you are set up for it (i.e. have the facilities and proper licensing), either of these is a great way to enhance your training income.

Regardless of which type or types of training you do, there will always be peaks and lulls throughout the year. Many people vacation in the summer while the kids are off school; your business may slow during that time. Business is likely to be sporadic during and closely following Christmas, but may well pick up three months later when all those cute holiday gift-pups start displaying puppy behavior problems.

Climate is another consideration. Depending on where you live and what type of training you do, the weather can seriously affect your business. I currently live in southern California. Because of the mild climate, outdoor classes run here almost year-round. In New York, where I'm originally from, not many people want to train in the rain and snow, so mid-winters are a definite down time for group classes, unless they are held indoors. Consider the climate you live in. Will it literally put a "damper" on your income? If having a steady income year-round is crucial, I would suggest holding a part-time job while you get your business going, and possibly even keeping it on a permanent basis. That way when training is slow, you'll still have a way to get by and pay the bills.

What Type of Training Will You Do?

Although we're focusing specifically on only one thing—pet dog training—there are still many different ways you can work with pet dogs. Here are a few of the most common:

Obedience

Some trainers choose to offer obedience instruction, and don't deal with behavior issues at all. There is nothing wrong with that. In fact, there is a real need for qualified obedience instructors who use positive methods. Obedience training can take place in a group class setting or one-on-one in the client's home (or in your office). In-home obedience training is usually done with the client present. Some trainers, however, set up a schedule where they work one-on-one with the dog a certain number of times per week. They follow up by getting together with the client periodically, so the client sees the progress being made and learns how to work with the dog themselves.

Group Classes

Should you choose to run group obedience classes, you will have some decisions to make. First, where will you train? If you work as an employee of a chain pet supply store or other large company, training space will probably be provided for you. Trainers may also give classes through small, local pet supply stores or veterinary clinics. In those cases, classes are held in the parking lot, or inside if space allows. Sign-up sheets are usually displayed on-site for potential clients to see. Some trainers lease space through their local Parks and Recreation Department. This offers the advantage of a nice park setting and the opportunity for your

7

class to be seen by bystanders, who might then sign up themselves. Most parks departments will even promote the classes for you. The tradeoff is that they take a percentage of your profits (which affects how many dogs you must have in class to make it worth your while financially). Other places to potentially hold classes include church parking lots, school gymnasiums or auditoriums, veterans halls, or even a friend's back yard. Consider the climate where you live, and whether the weather will permit you to train outdoors year-round. If not, an indoor facility might be more advantageous. You could even eventually opt to lease a space to create your own training facility.

Another class consideration is size. Some chain pet supply stores offer classes which enroll up to twenty dogs, with only one instructor. However, unless you are working with a few assistants, I would advise you to keep your class size small. When I teach group classes, I limit them to only six dogs. I don't work with an assistant, and feel that six dogs (and their assorted people) are all I can handle while still giving everyone the quality, hands-on attention they deserve. People really seem to appreciate that. If it's financially feasible, you could even offer "semi-private group classes" limited to, say, four dogs. I haven't seen this type of class advertised much, but when I have offered them, the response has been positive. Semi-private groups offer an alternative to those who can't or don't want to pay for an in-home, one-on-one visit, but don't want a large, impersonal group, either. And, that "exclusive" group label really appeals to certain people.

You will also have to decide what levels of obedience you will offer. Some trainers, especially when they're first starting out, offer basic obedience and nothing more. That's fine. The majority of dog owners would benefit greatly from training their dog in the basics, even if they never went further. Of course, you could

8

also offer intermediate and advanced classes. For more specific considerations regarding group classes, see *Group Class Tips*.

Puppy Kindergarten

A wonderful group class to offer is Puppy Kindergarten. The emphasis in puppy class is on socialization with other pups and people. A good puppy class will cover issues that most owners are dealing with, such as puppy nipping, chewing, jumping up and housebreaking. People are often relieved to find that their pup is not the only one! Classes should include handling and restraint exercises, which make future groomer and vet visits easier and help the puppy/owner bond. Students should be taught to manage situations and supervise so that pups don't get into trouble in the first place. Pups should be introduced to novel stimuli. And, "puppy pacifiers" such as the Kong and Buster Cube should be shown and explained (see *Tips - Products*). Many puppy classes also include an introduction to basic obedience. They are never too young to learn!

Traditional puppy classes start at four months of age. That's because sixteen weeks is the age at which the rabies vaccination is given. At that time, all vaccinations are considered complete. Many veterinarians feel that it is unsafe to have puppies around other dogs at all before that. However, the optimum window of socialization in dogs is between four and twelve weeks of age. It's not that a puppy can't be socialized after that, but before twelve weeks is when it is most effective. Many trainers, myself included, feel that as long as the pup is healthy and has had at least two rounds of vaccinations, they are eligible for puppy class. Naturally, you'll want to make sure the area you teach in is free of germs. For example, if your puppy class is held at a veterinary clinic, you'll want to make sure the floors are thoroughly disinfected before each class. You wouldn't hold a puppy class at a public park, since there would be a real threat of contracting diseases such as parvo or distemper from sick dogs who had been there before. If you choose to accept very young pups, you might want to bring the maximum age down a bit so that you don't end up with three-month-olds being overwhelmed by six-month-olds in play. For more on puppy class, see *Puppy Class Tips*.

Other types of group classes you could offer include trick training (see *Resources* for a great trick-training video set), clicker training —more on that later—one-topic classes (i.e. a four-week session on leashwork only) and "growl" classes, for dog-aggressive dogs. (Actually, many dogs in growl classes are more "dog-obnoxious," as my trainer friend Laura Bourhenne calls them, bullies, rather than truly dog-aggressive.) Growl classes are not usually given by novice trainers, but are something you might want to consider later on, as you gain confidence and experience. Other areas to consider learning about and possibly eventually teaching are agility, tracking and therapy work.

In-Home Training

Some trainers prefer to do only in-home training. They screen clients by phone, then go to their home to train. An in-home trainer might also accompany clients to a rescue or shelter to temperament-test potential adoptees, to ensure a good match.

The majority of my own practice is in-home training. I really enjoy the one-on-one interaction. So much progress can be made when it's just you, the client and that one dog you can concentrate on. There is more of a personal involvement with one-on-one training as opposed to a group class setting. Unfortunately, that can be a double-edged sword. On one hand, it's fascinating and rewarding to get into the dog's mind, observe owner-dog interactions, tweak the behavior modification program to fit the particular dogs' needs and see progress being made. On the other hand, when you have a difficult client (usually the people, not the dog), you're there one-on-one, lucky you. Developing good people skills is essential for any dog trainer. While it's important in a group setting, it is especially crucial in private training. Fortunately, the majority of clients are a pleasure to work with. (See *Resources* for books on dealing with difficult personality types.)

While some clients will call you to their home for private obedience training, more often, a behavior issue is involved. A "behavior issue" can be anything from separation anxiety (the dog getting stressed when the owner leaves), to jumping on the kids, to biting people. There are more behavior issues than I could possibly list here, and infinite variations on each. You will need to decide which issues you feel comfortable working with.

The first few years I trained, I did not work with aggressive dogs at all. There is absolutely nothing wrong with referring clients to another trainer who has more expertise in an area that you are uneasy with. In fact, it's the right thing to do for both the client and the dog's sake. Now I will work with dog-aggressive and people-aggressive dogs, but if it is a truly severe people-aggression case, I still might refer it to someone who specializes in that area.

If you're going to work with dog-dog aggression issues, consider whether you have a dog of your own who is "bombproof," i.e. does not react or become stressed no matter what is going on in the environment. It is much easier to desensitize dog-aggressive dogs to being around others if your own dog does not react to signs of aggression from them. Do you own or have access to a dog with that sort of temperament? If not, you can still work with dog-aggressive dogs, but it will be more difficult. (You will likely be desensitizing the dog-aggressive dog to dogs you encounter in public instead, which is more unpredictable, since it's harder to control the variables.)

How many sessions does in-home training take? That depends. A simple behavior issue such as housebreaking will probably take only one session to solve. By that I do not mean that the client's dog will never again have an "accident" in the house, but that in one session, you should be able to set up a management and housebreaking program that the client understands and is able to carry out without your further assistance. Other behavior issues such as fear and aggression will take longer. Just how long depends on the individual dog, and like so many other things, on the level of owner commitment.

You might, as many trainers do, decide to sell "packages" of sessions. For example, if you see that the issue will require more than a few visits, you could have the client pay you in advance for six sessions. This is often done with in-home clients who want a full obedience course for their dog but don't want to attend a group class. The package deal is not only financially good for you as a trainer, but also motivates the client to stick with the program. If you decide to offer package deals, have a contract ready which outlines the terms of your agreement. It is also a good idea to include a proviso which stipulates a date by which the sessions must be completed. Otherwise, you may end up with a client who perpetually postpones appointments, which affects the program's continuity. Learning how to deal with behavior issues takes time. In the next section we will discuss some ways to get started.

Board-And-Train

You might decide that rather than holding group classes or doing in-home training, you'd prefer to board and train dogs in your own home. Should you choose this option, the first thing to do is research the zoning laws in your area. The type of business you will be running may require a business license, and possibly a kennel license as well. Check with your local City Clerk's office for zoning restrictions and licensing requirements. Another consideration is how many dogs you can accommodate and how well you are set up to manage them. For example, some dogs will not get along well with others. Is your facility set up to keep them separated? Liability goes hand in hand with boarding. You are completely responsible for the welfare of the dogs in your care. On the positive side, board and train is a great way to get quality training time with a dog. Sometimes removing the dog from the home environment gives the dog a better chance to work through certain issues, especially ones that the owners are unwittingly contributing to. It's rewarding to see the joy on an owner's face when you show off how much progress their four-footed darling has made. Board and train can also be very satisfying on a financial level.

Other training alternatives include offering instruction at an established boarding facility, or at a shelter where your training will help the dogs to get adopted (more on shelter training later). All of the options mentioned so far presume that you are a one-person business. If you don't want to jump in with both feet, there are still other alternatives. You could work for an existing company, where you would be trained to teach group classes and possibly to do in-home training. In addition to local organizations, two national chains, PETsMART and PetCo, each have their own program to hire and educate new trainers (see *Resources*).

Don't let these considerations overwhelm you. You don't have to make any decisions right now, and you might well start out doing one thing and naturally move into doing another. In the next chapter, we'll look at specific ways to get started on your dog training education.

Getting An Education

Dog training has changed a lot over the last fifty years. Traditional obedience training involved force and coercion, and was not always pleasant for dogs or people. I'm happy to report that more and more trainers are now using fun, humane methods like lure-reward and clicker training. Lure-reward training uses food to lure the dog into position, and then to reward him. For example, a sitting dog follows a food treat which is moved from his nose down to the ground, until he is lying down. He is then given the food treat as a reward. Another method, clicker training, is becoming increasingly popular. Clicker training has been used with marine mammals and exotics for years. A small device called a clicker is used to mark the exact moment the dog is doing what we'd like. The click is then followed by a treat. Dogs learn quickly that click equals treat, so they begin to want to earn the click. The method is based on operant conditioning, and teaches dogs to think for themselves and to offer behaviors. It is very effective for teaching obedience and modifying behavior, and is also an excellent method for teaching tricks. The *Resource* section includes books which explain clicker training in depth. Once you read up and try out the techniques with your own fur-kids, you may be hooked!

There are still many trainers who use punishment-based methods, though I haven't yet come across anyone who calls themselves a "negative" or "punishment-based trainer." (Gee, what kind of advertising would *that* make for: *"Our motto is, 'Jerk A Bit 'Till They Submit!'"*) Some trainers employ correction-based methods, ranging from mild to harsh. Others use a combination of corrections and praise, and refer to themselves as "balanced trainers." You will cross paths with trainers from all philosophies.

15

Resist the urge to think of them as right or wrong, or to judge them. Everyone has methods that work best for them. You can learn something from everyone, even if it's only to decide what you *don't* want to incorporate into your own training.

~ * ~ * ~ * ~ * ~ * ~ * ~ * ~ * ~ * ~ * ~ * ~ * ~ * ~

As previously mentioned, my goal is not to teach you *how* to train dogs. I do, however, want to guide you to as many resources as possible to get the necessary education so you can begin your training career. It might surprise you to know there is no degree or license necessary to become a pet dog trainer. Your Uncle Bob could hang out a shingle tomorrow, announcing Uncle Bobby's Dog Training. Frightening, isn't it? The Association of Pet Dog Trainers (APDT) (more on this wonderful organization in a moment) is currently rectifying that problem by designing a certification program for dog trainers that will be recognized worldwide.

Certification aside, dog trainers are largely a self-educated bunch. Fortunately, there are now many avenues to getting a great training education:

Publications

Books and online information, videos and seminars are great resources to kick-start your education. In the *Resources* section, I have listed some of the best dog training books and videos on the market. They all promote training with positive methods. Some are basic, geared toward the general public, while others are more appropriate for the serious student of canine behavior. Not all of them are about how to train dogs, either. For example, a few offer advice on how to deal with people; another discusses how to recognize stress signals in dogs; some describe breed characteristics. All of these topics are extremely helpful to your becoming a well-rounded, effective trainer. Make it your business to search out books on a wide variety of dog-related topics. Read non-dog-related books as well, on subjects such as training other types of animals, working with people, family dynamics and small business management. Everything you read will be helpful in some way.

In the *Resources* section, you will find a magazine called *The Whole Dog Journal.* This monthly publication has consistently top-quality articles on training techniques, canine health and nutrition, and comparisons and ratings of training books, equipment, dog toys, foods and more. Another helpful feature of the magazine is the opportunity to order back issues. If you find that you lack knowledge in a certain area and can't find the latest research, i.e. treating canine noise phobias, chances are there's a back issue that covers just that topic. All I can say is, I just renewed my subscription for another two years. It's that good!

Association of Pet Dog Trainers (APDT)

One of the best things you can possibly do in your quest for knowledge is to join the Association of Pet Dog Trainers (APDT). Founded by Dr. Ian Dunbar, a pioneer in positive training methods, the organization focuses on promoting positive training techniques and on the ongoing education of its members. You need not be a professional trainer to join. Membership is inexpensive, and the yearly dues entitle you to receive the organization's newsletter, discounts on conferences, and to join the on-line mailing list. The newsletter alone is worth it. It is filled with not only news about the organization and its members, but also useful training articles, brainstorming on how to solve behavior issues and more.

The internet mailing list, APDT-L, is an amazing resource which is free to APDT members. Some of the top trainers in the world subscribe, and are generous enough to give advice and share their experiences. Trainers at all levels share tips on common behavior issues; members post case histories and receive feedback and suggestions; support and encouragement is offered to those who need it; and information is shared about training techniques and upcoming seminars.

Speaking of seminars, the APDT Annual Educational Conference is something you do not want to miss. This five-day extravaganza immerses trainers in seminars and workshops taught by some of the world's top trainers. It affords the opportunity to meet and learn from some of the folks whose books you've been reading and to network with other trainers from around the world. The conference also hosts a large trade show where you can check out the latest training equipment, get bargains on all kinds of great dog-related stuff, and attend live demonstrations throughout the day.

I can tell you first-hand that no matter what your level of knowledge, from novice to experienced, the APDT will be an incredible help to you. If this sounds like a commercial message for the APDT, well, it is. I credit the organization's seminars, internet list, newsletters and contacts with upgrading my own education immensely, and it continues to this day. I truly believe that the APDT is one of the most valuable resources out there for dog trainers today. (See *Resources* for contact info.)

Internet Resources

There is a wealth of information on the internet regarding training, some extremely helpful and some...well, not so helpful. Use your own judgment and remember that just because it's in print doesn't mean it's true. Anyone can put up a web page. There are, however, some excellent web sites out there, chock full of useful information. Some store the best posts from mailing lists (where posts are received as e-mail) so anyone can access them. Others list canine behavior problems individually, with ideas on how to solve them. A few of these sites are listed in *Resources*. You will find many more on your own. There are also web sites which will alert you to upcoming seminars and workshops. Besides the APDT web site, Puppyworks is a great one (see *Resources* for both). Both sites offer information about seminars given by well-known professional trainers, the majority of whom use positive methods. Puppyworks also sells videotapes of seminars, which is especially helpful if you can't travel. If there are no seminars in your area, consider organizing one yourself. If there is a group or trainer from whom you would like to learn, contact them and ask what it would take to organize a seminar. Many trainers travel the country and are available to do lectures and workshops.

There are many excellent internet mailing lists which specifically address training issues. When you subscribe to one, you will receive the posts as e-mail. (Some groups allow you to view the posts at a web site instead.) Many lists are high-volume, meaning you might get upwards of fifty e-mails a day. Many are worth it! One of my favorites is Clicker Solutions, which focuses exclusively on clicker training. There are many excellent trainers there and loads of great information. I often find myself copying and pasting posts from both the Clicker Solutions and the APDT lists into word processing files for future reference.

Other lists cover specific topics such as aggression. A good place to start your search is at Yahoo Groups (see *Resources*). Just do a search for "dog" or "canine" (without the quotations). A selection of lists will come up, along with a description of each. Try them out. You can easily unsubscribe if they're not a good fit, and you might just get a wealth of helpful information, absolutely free.

Apprenticeship

Regardless of how much theoretical knowledge you gain, you will still need hands-on experience. One way to get it is to find a knowledgeable, positive trainer in your area who is willing to take you on as an apprentice. Experienced trainers will often allow an apprentice to assist in group classes. Some will require that you bring your own dog through their class first. This arrangement is advantageous for you both; you get first-hand experience with their training techniques, and you both get a feel for whether your personalities and training styles click. Don't be discouraged if you find that some trainers are less than friendly when approached. Unfortunately, there are those trainers who take the element of competition very seriously and have less than helpful attitudes toward other trainers. Usually the folks who feel that way are insecure themselves. Keep looking. Experienced, secure trainers who understand that there are enough dogs with behavior problems to go around and that the world needs more positive trainers are out there. You will find one who is willing to help you along. A good place to start is at the APDT web site. Click on "Trainer Search" to find contact information for trainers in your area.

Note: If you are planning to teach group classes, observe as many different trainers teach a class as possible. You might not like everything they do, but you will pick up a lot by just watching them. You might learn new techniques, or gain insights on ways to manage a class or how to better relate to students.

Once you become acquainted with an experienced trainer, they might invite you to trainer meetings. Often referred to as Trainer Roundtables, these meetings are for trainers to network, and to share ideas and information. Your mentor might also be able to provide information on events in your area that are not widely advertised. Depending on the trainer you apprentice with, you could eventually become a paid assistant in their classes, teach classes for them, and/or work into doing in-home training for their company.

Schools

There are degrees you can earn which would be helpful in working with dogs, such as those in Applied Psychology, Ethology and Zoology, and Applied Animal Behavior. Most require undergraduate work in areas like biology and other sciences. You could go on to get a Masters and even a Ph.D. If this interests you, start with your local university and research opportunities online. Again, keep in mind that you can still be a fantastic dog trainer without a single degree.

The title of "Behaviorist" is a specific credential. It includes a Ph.D. in one of a few specific areas. Without going into exactly what makes an actual Behaviorist, allow me to air a pet peeve. Some trainers promote themselves as a "Behaviorist" without having the necessary academic qualifications. This is unethical! One who specializes in behavior issues may, however, call themselves a Behavior Specialist or Pet Behavior Counselor.

San Francisco SPCA

There is an excellent training course offered through the San Francisco SPCA, taught by renowned trainer/author Jean Donaldson. The organization's web site calls the CTC (Certificate in Training and Counseling) program, "a six-week, full-time course designed to provide a thorough, well-rounded education in pet dog training and behavior counseling. The curriculum combines lecture, video, demonstration and round-table discussion with hands-on training as well as rehearsal of instructing and interviewing skills." Students work with shelter dogs, complete homework assignments and get lots of personal feedback. If you can spare the expense and the six weeks away from home, this might be the school for you. (See *Resources* for contact info.)

Moorpark College

Another excellent opportunity exists to gain training skills, not with dogs, but with exotic animals. Moorpark College, located in Southern California, offers a unique opportunity for students to work with exotic animals ranging from marmosets to elephants, alligators to big cats. Students come from all over the world to work with the 150 animals in the EATM (Exotic Animal Training and Management) program. (*Note*: Students are expected to work many nights and weekends; the program is very intense.) Although dogs are not part of the program, working with exotics will give you invaluable training in operant conditioning and make you a much better dog trainer. You could even earn an Associate in Science degree. (See *Resources* for contact info.)

PETsMART/PetCo

Some of the larger, nationwide dog training companies periodically place ads for new trainers. This can be an excellent opportunity for you to learn to train dogs. These companies will put you through an entire training course, usually at little or no cost to you. PETsMART recently revamped their program to incorporate more positive methods, including clicker training. PetCo's training is done through ABTA (Animal Behavior and Training Associates). See *Resources* for contact info for both.

Dog Training Academies

You have probably seen ads in national magazines, on the internet and elsewhere for Such-and-Such "Dog Training Academy." Proceed with caution! Some are good, while others are less than wonderful and do not use humane methods. Most are very expensive, and the certification you earn through them is not nationally recognized. When researching a school, keep in mind that a good dog training curriculum should include an overview of training, theory, breed characteristics, genetics, social development, behavior issues and business considerations. It should also offer plenty of hands-on experience with a variety of dogs. Ask for contact information for a few students who have attended the school. Get their feedback. Ask too whether you can observe a class where the students are actually training dogs. Remember, if there is anything you're not comfortable with, don't assume the instructors are right. They might simply be using methods that you are not interested in using. Keep looking.

So You Want To Be A Dog Trainer

Gimme Shelter

An excellent way to gain invaluable hands-on experience with dogs is to volunteer at your local shelter. I strongly urge you to do this, regardless of whether you find an individual trainer or company to tutor you. There is no education like the one you will get handling and training the variety of dogs that come into a shelter. I spent many hours a week for a few years at my local city shelter, first as a volunteer and then as Volunteer Coordinator, training other volunteers. It was an amazing experience that improved my skills on many levels. Shelter work will allow you to gain skill in handling dogs, reading canine body language and dealing with the public. You might also make contacts which will help your future career.

You might find that the shelter you want to volunteer at already has a trainer present. Great! Observe what they do. You may or may not agree with their methods, but you can learn something regardless. Rather than announcing yourself as a potential trainer, go in with a low-key, helpful, willing-to-do-anything attitude. While some shelters have structured programs to train new volunteers, others have none. Either way, learn and respect the procedures for dealing with the animals and the public.

Keep in mind that you may experience some emotional difficulty regarding attachment to the dogs, especially if the shelter euthanizes those who are not adopted. Just remember, the help you are giving the dogs and the experience you are getting is invaluable.

There are excellent resources available to those who are specifically interested in working with shelter dogs. Trainer Sue Sternberg has authored booklets which specifically address temperament testing and training shelter dogs, how to choose a dog from a shelter and more. (See *Resources/Other Publications*.) There is also an internet discussion list devoted specifically to those who train at shelters. It is a great resource for information and support, and is included in the *Resources* section.

Rescue Me

Closely related to working with shelter dogs, is working with a rescue group. Some groups are breed-specific, while others rescue mixed breeds. Get a list of local rescues. Some hold adoption days at local parks or pet supply stores. Stop by and observe what goes on, and if you're interested, introduce yourself. Explain that you are a novice trainer and would like to help. Most groups will be happy to take advantage. The fact that you're a new trainer shouldn't be a hindrance. After all, their dogs will be receiving free training, which only makes them more adoptable.

~ * ~ * ~ * ~ * ~ * ~ * ~ * ~ * ~ * ~ * ~ * ~ * ~

So is your head spinning yet? There certainly are a lot of educational opportunities out there! The good news is that not only are there more resources than ever available to those wanting to train pet dogs, but that many of those resources are based on positive training methods.

Suggested Research Topics

When you first start reading books and watching videos, the sheer volume of information might seem overwhelming. Don't expect to learn everything at once. Tackle one subject at a time. Research each one not only in books, but by reading articles on the internet and speaking with other trainers. Here are a few to start with:

Breeds

No one expects you to be familiar with every dog breed in existence. Besides, no matter how well you know the common ones, you will inevitably come across a few you've never heard of. I recently saw two Entelbuchers, in separate families living in the same neighborhood, within one month. What are the chances? (The second client was impressed with how much I knew about this rare breed—hehee!) You will find in your area, certain breeds are popular. My business serves a family-oriented community where many people have Labrador Retrievers. It also covers a more rural area, where I see many Australian Cattle Dogs and other "ranch" type breeds. Some trainers might see more hound breeds or pit bull types, depending on their geographic location. Start with the most popular breeds in your area. Research what they were bred for, what medical problems they're prone to, what their temperament is like, whether they make good family dogs, require a lot of exercise, etc. If you do this before each in-home appointment, you will be that much better prepared to answer questions and will impress the client with your knowledge. Knowing the breed groupings and characteristics of each will also help in your training. For example, Beagles are scenthounds, so you know getting a super-reliable recall will be important. After all, a Beagle will likely be distracted by some fascinating

27

scent on the ground while you're calling. You'll also know to tell the client to keep their garbage can well covered!

Stages of Development

You will be a much more effective trainer, particularly with pups and younger dogs, if you are familiar with their stages of physical and behavioral development. For example, if you know the period for optimum socialization with other dogs, people and novel stimuli is between four and twelve weeks of age, you could give clients advice regarding exposing their pups to those things safely during that period. If you know dogs teethe between four and seven months of age, you'll be prepared to offer solutions to a client whose pup is going through that phase. Knowing when sexual maturity occurs can help to explain dog-to-dog aggression issues. There are countless ways your knowledge of stages of canine development will come in handy.

Behavior Issues

There is no way to prepare for every individual behavior issue that will arise. Even the ones you're familiar with will have variations, and how you deal them will be modified as you go along. However, some issues are common and will almost certainly present themselves. You should have a basic idea of how to deal with them:

Housebreaking/Crate training
Jumping on people
Barking
Nipping
Destruction/Chewing
Digging

Yard escaping
Counter-surfing
Door darting
Submissive urination
Rehoming issues (special needs of rescue dogs)
Integrating a new dog into a home with existing dogs/other pets
Resource guarding (guarding objects/food/locations/people)
Canine-child interactions
Fear issues
Dog-dog fighting within the home
Separation anxiety
... and, if you're going to handle them:
Aggression toward people
Aggression toward other dogs
(and the basis and treatment for all sub-categories of aggression)

Obedience Training

Learn how to train these basics:

Attention
Sit
Stay
Down
Come (also referred to as the "recall")
Loose Leash-Walking or Heel
Leave It

Canine Body Language

It is crucial that you get familiar and comfortable with canine body language. You will be much more efficient at assisting owners if you can tell (and teach them how to tell) when their dog is stressed, afraid, becoming frustrated, reactive, potentially aggressive, or displaying a variety of other emotions. I suggest you read Turid Rugaas' wonderful book, *On Talking Terms with Dogs: Calming Signals* (see *Resources*), which outlines common stress signals in dogs that most people are not aware of. These signals are also used by dogs to calm other dogs (and sometimes people). Some can even be used by humans to calm dogs. Remember too that working with shelter dogs is an excellent way to get a crash course in canine body language.

Natural Remedies

We, as dog trainers, are not legally permitted to prescribe medication. Only a veterinarian can do that. Should you feel a dog is in need of medication, refer the client to their vet. It is, however, useful to have a good, working knowledge of not only common drugs and medications prescribed for canines, but of natural remedies as well. Dogs with all types of behavior issues can be helped by modalities such as Ttouch (a form of massage), acupressure, Bach Flowers, homeopathic remedies, nutritional therapy and more. See *Resources* for books on these topics.

Building Confidence

A friend of mine is just starting her dog training career. She has read all the right books, watched step-by-step videos and practiced with her own dogs. She works part time at a shelter, so she has experience working with a variety of breeds and temperaments. She would be a good professional trainer. The trouble is, she lacks the confidence to make the leap to training as an actual job. She feels hesitant about charging money for her skills, which she feels may be underdeveloped, especially compared to other trainers in her area. You may find yourself in a similar situation. If so, here are some suggestions to bridge the gap and allow you to feel better about charging for your services:

Phone a Friend

Enlist a friend to help you set up a mock training session. The friend should call you just as a client would, so you can practice your phone skills. Set up an appointment. Arrive with the understanding that as long as you are there, you are the trainer and your friend is the client—no "friend talk" until afterward. Do everything just as you would if this were an actual client. Go through the session, ask questions, chat, work with the dog, and recommend a program for the client to continue working with. Schedule another appointment if necessary. Then get feedback from your friend. Ask whether the suggestions you made were helpful, whether you were clear, and to offer any other comments they feel might be helpful. Doing this type of mock session may help you to work out some of the kinks before taking on actual clients, and give you the confidence to do so.

To the Rescue!

Contact a rescue group and offer to do a free in-home training session for anyone who adopts a dog from them. Or, offer a free group class to adopters. Since you're not charging for your services, you won't feel so pressured. Although you won't have to keep sessions to a strict time frame, it will be good practice for getting your pacing down, as your "real" clients will be paying by the hour.

Another type of service you could offer is a free group class for the volunteers of a rescue group. Each volunteer could take a rescue dog through your class. This accomplishes three things: the dogs get training, which makes them more adoptable; the volunteers learn valuable training skills, which they can then use with any dog who comes into the rescue; and you develop your skills and build confidence. A great perk that goes with offering any of these services to a rescue group, is that once you do start charging for your services, you will probably get referrals from them. Be sure to offer their adopters a discount!

Rent-A-Trainer

Hire an experienced trainer to come along on an actual in-home visit. Explain to the client in advance that your friend is coming along to help, because he/she is a trainer as well and may have some additional input. The client shouldn't mind. After all, they're getting two trainers for the price of one! The trainer should observe the session quietly, offer helpful advice when appropriate, then give constructive criticism and feedback in private afterwards. Try not to be nervous because of the monitoring. The trainer is there to help and their positive feedback should make you feel more confident.

When All Else Fails

Though it's not likely, imagine that the worst happens: You go on a session and are faced with a problem you simply can not resolve. It's something you weren't expecting, or maybe it's a subject you are familiar with but have never seen presented in quite this way. Relax. It's perfectly okay to tell the client this is something that really has you stumped. If there are other issues that were worked through during the session, i.e. this is one of many and not the sole reason you are there, offer to consult with other trainers/resources and phone them back regarding a working solution for the problem. If it is the entire reason for your visit, as a last resort, offer to refund their money and apologize for not being able to help them with this particular matter. If you know someone who is more experienced with that particular issue, refer the client to them. It may be awkward, but it is not the end of the world. And, it will probably never happen. In fact, you might be surprised to discover how much you *do* know. As you go along, your skills will improve. You will develop confidence and get better at dealing with novel situations. You *will* be a good trainer!

Take your time, get some experience, and don't feel cowed by or compare yourself with other trainers. They may have been in the business for over thirty years, but the question is, what have they learned during that time? Are they out there going to seminars and reading books, keeping their mind open to new information? Or are they stuck in the same old ways of training that were standard when they started out? It may well be that even with only a few years experience, trainers who uses positive methods and are always learning and honing their skills can far surpass more experienced trainers. Remember: *The best trainers are those who never stop learning!*

33

Setting Up Your Business

The Red Tape, Nuts N' Bolts Business Stuff

If you choose to become an employee of an established training company, you won't have to deal with some of the issues mentioned in this chapter. The responsibility for advertising, record-keeping and other company business will fall to your employer. Your responsibility will be to learn their methods and curriculum and do a good job training.

If you choose to operate as a one-person company, there are some important preparations to make. I'm going to assume you've been reading books and doing research, have gotten some hands-on experience and feel confident in launching your dog training career. Now, let's move on to the nitty-gritty of business setup.

DBA (Doing Business As)

Most states require that when you start up a new business, you place a DBA (Doing Business As) notice in the newspaper. This small, inexpensive classified ad tells the world you are operating as Such-and-Such business. The newspaper will have a search done before placing the ad, to ensure that no one else in your city is already using that name. The good thing about it is, once your ad is placed, no one in your city can use the name you have chosen, either. Call your local newspaper for more information.

Note: Your business name should reflect what you're all about. For example, "Gentle Guidance" suggests gentle methods and helpful instruction. "Who's The Boss Dog Training," on the other

35

hand, reflects a mindset based on the old "dominance" model of behavior. Also, stay away from generic names. There are countless "K-9 Trainer" type names out there. Make yours stand out so people take notice.

Licensing

Some cities or states require that you obtain a business license regardless of the type of business you run or the number of employees you have. Others do not require a one-person business working out of the home to carry a business license. Call your local County Clerk's office to find out what the regulations are in your area.

Resale

If you plan to sell training or other supplies to your clients, you will need a resale license. Depending on where you live, you may be required to charge and then annually report sales tax on those items. Check with your State Board of Equalization for regulations in your area.

Banking

It is to your advantage to set up a separate checking account for your business. Doing so keeps income and expenditures separate from your personal accounts, which makes keeping track for tax purposes simpler. It also looks more professional to have people make checks out to a business, rather than to you personally. Order an authorization stamp through your bank or rubber stamp store to endorse the checks you receive. It should include your business name, bank and account number. After all, you *will* eventually have too many checks to keep signing them manually!

Insurance

Regardless of how small your client base is to begin with, you should carry liability insurance. You might be an incredible trainer, but this is the real world and hey, dog poop happens. There was a case recently where a well-known, very experienced behaviorist was working with a client's dog in public. The dog severely bit a passerby. The man sued the behaviorist for a million dollars—and won. Although this sort of thing doesn't happen often, it can and does happen.

If you plan to teach classes through your local city or county's Parks and Recreation Department, you might find they require you to carry a million-dollar liability policy. They might also ask that you list them as co-insured. This is standard practice, and protects them in the event someone sues. Insurance is inexpensive and well worth the cost. Check out exactly what the policy covers. Does it insure only you or the place where you give classes as well? Does it cover medical expenses? Two carriers who will insure dog trainers are listed in *Resources*.

Setting Fees

Whether you opt to do group classes, private, in-home training or a combination of both, you must set your fees. There are no real guidelines for this, as fees vary greatly from region to region. Rates are generally higher in heavily populated, urban areas and less so in remote regions. Call around to trainers in your area to find out what their fees are. You don't need to announce yourself as a trainer, but could inquire instead as an interested party. If you don't feel comfortable doing so, ask a friend to call around for you.

Don't try to beat the competition. Cheap is not always more attractive to potential customers. In fact, there is a strange phenomenon whereby people think if it costs more, it's worth more. If you're doing group classes, calculate what you must charge per person based on the number of dogs in class, to arrive at the figure you need to make. One hour-long group class lesson nets me approximately the same as one hour-long in-home session. Your mileage may vary depending on your class size, venue and geographic location. When calculating, be sure to include the time you spend on class preparation, i.e., creating lesson plans and homeworks.

For in-home training, be sure to take travel time into account. Decide on a basic fee to cover a specific distance range. For example, let's say you charge fifty dollars per hour, which applies to visiting any home within fifteen miles from yours. Now, take a map and draw a circle with a fifteen mile radius, with your home as the center point. Draw another circle outside of that one, with an additional ten mile radius. Anything that falls between the first circle and the second will require, for example, an additional ten dollar travel fee. Keep drawing circles up to the distance you are willing to travel. That way when someone inquires about an area you're not familiar with, you can easily refer to the map and let them know whether you service that area and if so, what the charge would be.

The Home Office

Since you are just starting out, I'm going to assume that your base of operations will be your home, as opposed to a rented training space. Designate a room or area of a room as your home office. The most helpful "office supply" to have in this space is a personal computer with a high quality laser printer.

Purchase a financial program aimed at small business owners. This program will allow you to enter transactions such as payments from clients (income) and anything you spend money on for the business (expenses). Record-keeping is essential for tax purposes, and a computerized program makes it easy to input and separate items into categories. For example, expenditures could be broken down into Advertising, Training Equipment, Office Supplies and so forth. I personally use Quicken Home & Office. It's simple to set up and use, and allows you to create charts and graphs so you can track your financial progress.

While we're on the subject of finances, get in the habit of saving your receipts for anything and everything that is business-related. If you use your vehicle to drive to clients' homes, part of your car-related expenses are deductible; if you discuss dog training over lunch with your mentor, that meal is deductible; so are your training supplies. Having a home office may allow you to write off part of your mortgage, phone bills and utilities. Get a list from your tax consultant of what is potentially deductible. Keep a file of your bills and receipts. Remember that with your own business, you are completely responsible for keeping careful track of all your income and expenses. Once your income begins to grow, you might want to consider paying your taxes quarterly rather than annually, so the payment isn't overwhelming.

Another helpful tool to have is a database program. Any standard database program will allow you to keep clients' addresses and contact information on file. It will also allow you to print address labels, which is helpful should you decide to do a mass mailing such as holiday cards or special incentives. One last program you'll need is a word processing program such as Word, so you can print letters, contracts, attendance sheets, lesson plans, homework for group class and handouts.

In addition to a computer, you will need a phone with a reliable answering machine. Spend the few extra dollars to purchase a quality unit. There is nothing more disconcerting than having someone tell you they've left repeated messages and have been waiting for a return call, when you've never even received the messages. You're then left wondering how many other potential clients' calls you've missed.

Dedicating a second phone line to your business is best, but if necessary, your main house line can be used for business as well. Just be sure the outgoing message sounds friendly and professional, and when you answer the phone, you use your business name spoken in a professional manner. (Just warn your friends and family that the strangely business-like person is actually you, or they'll think they have the wrong number.)

On The Road

On the subject of phones, while you're on the road, a cell phone is essential. It will allow you to let clients know when you've been delayed, to check your messages and return calls promptly, and of course, to call for help in an emergency. A cell phone is absolutely worth the expense. Besides, its business use is tax-deductible.

You will also want to have a date book with you at all times so when you knock the socks off those clients and they want you back for another appointment, you can jot down the date and time.

Business Supplies Shopping List

Fax machine
Paper for printer/fax
Loose-leaf binder
Telephone message pads
Stapler
Scotch tape
Three-hole punch
Scissors
Pens
Pen holder
Post-it notes
Envelopes
Computer disks
(to back up data)
Return address labels
Bulletin board
Office wall calendar/
Markers

Preparing Your Printed Matter

We're almost there. Before you start advertising, though, let's prepare some important printed matter:

Contracts

Whether you do in-home training or group classes, you should have clients sign a contract. When I teach group classes, I send out a contract in advance and ask that it be signed and returned along with payment to hold the student's place in class. Many trainers have all their private clients sign an agreement before any training takes place, regardless of whether the client does one session or ten. This is a good practice.

A contract should spell out clearly and concisely what services the client is entitled to receive, what your refund policy is, and should absolve you (at least on paper) of any liability that is not due to your own negligence. I say "at least on paper" because the truth of the matter is, a contract might not actually stand up in court. It might, however, lead the client to feel less inclined to sue once it's been signed. As far as refunds are concerned, although my contract states that none will be given after the first group class commences, I have actually given refunds to clients who had extenuating circumstances. But, I like the fact that the contract gives me the right to *not* refund monies if I so choose.

I have included a copy of my liability contract in the *Preparation for Group Class* chapter. It is just one example of a usable contract. Feel free to incorporate any part of it that you like in to your own form. I would suggest, however, that you have a lawyer review any contract before using it.

Handouts

Client handouts are usually a one-sheet summary regarding a specific topic. For example, I have handouts titled *Basic Principles of Positive Training, Crate Training, An Introduction to Clicker Training, Suggested Reading List, How to Stuff a Kong (Or, Take This Kong and Stuff It!)* (more on Kongs later), *Resource Guarding* and *Leadership*, among others. Whether in class or in the home, clients can be nervous or distracted, and might not retain all the information you want to impart. It's useful to leave something in print for them to refer to. Handouts are also helpful for filling in any details you may have forgotten to mention. Topics may be general or linked specifically to holidays, such as the dangers of holiday plants, ornaments and foods (i.e. chocolate), or dealing with noise-phobias on the Fourth of July holiday.

Homework Assignments

Another type of handout you will need if you plan to give group classes is the homework assignment. A good homework sheet reviews what was taught in class, touches on key points about training the behavior, and offers suggestions on how students should work with their dogs until the next class. For example, if a food lure was used to train "Down," the handout might review the luring process, discuss how to fade the food lure and give specific directions on when, where and how long to practice at each session so the behavior becomes fluent.

Form Letters

If you plan to do group classes and prefer that people sign up in advance, have a form letter prepared to send out along with the contract. See *Group Class/Preparation* for a sample letter.

Coupons

Another printed handout to consider is the coupon. Everyone loves a bargain! Though you don't want to sell your services too cheaply, offering a one-time, ten-percent discount on a private session or group class won't hurt and might well draw in new clients. Coupons may be offered any time of year, or be tied in with a specific holiday or event. You could also present your current clients with an incentive coupon that offers, for example, twenty-five percent off a future session for every client they refer to you. And of course, discount coupons could go to shelters and rescue groups as well.

Now you've got your business set up, your policies in place and your printed matter prepared. Next stop, Advertising!

Advertising Essentials

It's time to let the world know just how much they want your services. Regardless of how small your initial advertising budget is, two things you'll need immediately are brochures and business cards.

Brochures

Brochures need not be expensive to produce. They do not require fancy paper or lots of color. I designed my own brochure using the PageMaker program on my personal computer. The first year I was in business, I simply printed out as many as were needed at the time. It was a two-sided, tri-fold design with simple black text on 8.5" x 11" pastel-colored paper. It looked professional, clean and clear, including the black and white photo on the cover. Years later, I still use the same basic design with slight modifications. My local print shop takes the file, saved on disk, and runs off as many copies as I need on plain pastel paper.

If you can afford to reproduce a color photo on the front of your brochure, great. If not, don't worry. A black and white brochure can look just as attractive. You could eventually go to color photos, glossy paper or heavier card-stock if you prefer, but there is no need to spend a lot of money at the beginning. As long as the brochure looks professional, it will get people's attention. Besides, it's what's written inside that will make them want to call you.

Note: If you don't already have one, start designing a logo to represent your business. Your logo should appear on your business cards, brochures, stationary and anything else you present to the public, if space allows. Keep the lines clean and simple. If you are not artistically inclined, get a friend to help or spend the money on a graphic designer. It's important that the logo look professional.

Keep the front cover of your brochure eye-catching and simple. You could incorporate an attractive photo of yourself with a dog or dogs, training or just hanging out, or even a cute photo of a dog alone or with a child. The brochure cover should display your business name and contact information, along with a brief announcement of what you do. The front of my brochure, for example, says *"Gentle Guidance"* with my logo just above it, then "Training" in block letters. Underneath that is my catch phrase, "For Dogs and Their People." There is a close-up, friendly-looking photo of myself and a Malamute mix, our heads tilted together affectionately. All it says directly under the photo is "Behavior Specialist." It then lists, on one line each, "Private, In-Home Training/Behavior Modification/Obedience/Puppy Kindergarten." My name and phone number appear at the bottom, along with a small line saying "Member, Association Pet Dog Trainers (APDT)." That might sound like a lot of text, but it's really not. It's spaced out nicely and doesn't look cluttered. Keep the cover simple. There's plenty of space inside to explain what you do and why you are the best person for the job.

Inside the brochure, describe the services you provide. Don't just list what you do. Make the text really zing! Let people know how you can specifically help them. You might want to mention some common behavior/training issues, so people see them and think, "Ah, that's just what my dog needs help with!" The first inside panel of my brochure lists common behavior problems, then says at the bottom, "...And Most Importantly...Your Dog's Specific Needs!" (I figure if I haven't mentioned their dog's individual issue, I still have it covered.) The center panel talks about my training philosophy, emphasizing that I train using positive methods, which are just as (and sometimes more) effective as traditional methods, but are more pleasant for both dog and owner. Be sure to let people know what's so special about you and your training, and why you're the best choice over any other trainer they could just as easily call.

Note: As far as brochure design, I'm partial to the tri-fold. Some people prefer to use a third-of-a-page, heavy stock one-sheet. These are tall, sturdy cards that sometimes have text on the back as well. Either way, be sure your brochure fits into a standard brochure stand. After all, it will eventually find its way to countertops all over your neighborhood!

My last inside panel offers a mini-biography/resume, which lists pertinent experience and qualifications. If you have experience volunteering with a shelter, belong to any dog-related associations, have held dog-related jobs or have an applicable degree or certification, here's where you should tell the world. Don't be shy, but don't toot your own horn too much, either. I saw a flyer once where the entire three inside panels were covered with the trainer's qualifications and experience. Extensive as they were, there was not a word about how he could help the potential client's dog! Find a balance. If you don't have much experience, that's okay. Don't lie about your qualifications, but do play up your good points. Have you always had a way with shy dogs? Great! Someone out there has a shy dog who would love to meet you. Did you ever do family counseling? Very applicable—you have a way not only with dogs, but with people. Even if you have no dog-related experience, list the things about you personally that will make people remember and want to call you.

Including a warm, friendly touch can help distinguish your brochure from all the cold, business-like ones out there. Mine has a tag at the end of the bio section that says, "Nicole is motivated by a true love of canines, and it shows. Her patience, kindness and sense of humor makes training fun and easy for both dog and owner." The idea is for people to understand that not only am I likely to treat their dog well, but that I will be patient with them too. They come away feeling that the experience will be pleasant for everyone—and it will!

Don't list prices on your brochure (it doesn't look professional and besides, you might want to adjust them), but do mention any special ongoing offers. For example, "One free in-home session when you register for Group Obedience Class." If you offer specific training programs, now is the time to talk about them. Most trainers in my area sell "package deals" where you have to purchase a block of six to eight sessions. My brochure boasts the alternative, "Go lesson by lesson—get as many private sessions as *you* need." Again, I'm telling the public what sets me apart, and why it's to their advantage to choose me.

As you build a clientele, you may want to include testimonials in your brochure. Testimonials are free, rave reviews that will make others want to have the kind of training experience these folks have had with you. I don't include testimonials in my brochure because it's already in danger of becoming overcrowded, but if you've got them and have space, use them. I do have one simple oval on the back of the last panel that frames the words, "Referred by more local vets, groomers and pet stores than any other trainer!" Don't include this sort of thing if it's not true, but if it is, don't feel silly about letting people know. Things like that tell the prospective client that professionals in the industry think enough of you to refer clients—a valuable endorsement of your services.

Business Cards

Next, you'll need a business card. It should include the name of your business, your logo, a brief line or two stating what you do, and your contact information. That's it. Though there is an infinite variety of business card designs available, ranging from plain black text on white card stock to multi-colored photos on a holographic background, keep it simple. Remember, you want it to look professional but not to cost you an arm and a leg. Rather than getting into the many ways you can design a business card, I would like to point you toward an excellent book called *How To Market Your Dog Training Business*, by Lisa K. Wilson. It was a great help to me when I started out. Wilson gives useful, specific information on designing business cards, brochures, newsletters and mailers, along with samples of each. She also details and gives sample letters of introduction, newsletters, news releases and more. (See *Resources*.) Once you've designed your business card, you can either print them on your home computer using one of the many programs and card sheets available, or bring the design to your local print shop for larger quantities.

Keep business cards with you at all times. They come in handy at get-togethers, or just about anywhere you run into someone and start talking dogs. Always leave a few cards with clients so they can keep one and pass the others along.

All The News That's Fit To Print

The Print Ad

Print ads run the gamut from inexpensive to wildly pricey. Some will generate a lot of business, while others will just sit there looking pretty. Research publications in your area and inquire about their advertising rates. Consider local newspapers, buy-lines type papers, small neighborhood publications and regional magazines. Be as specific to the area that your business serves as possible. Remember, you will get calls from people in all areas served by that publication. Decide how far you will travel and place your ads accordingly.

There are two main types of ad: a classified, text-only listing, and a display ad. Though a display ad is larger and allows for photos, there is nothing wrong with starting out with a classified ad. The advantage of classified ads is that they are less expensive, so you can afford to run them more often. Find out what your local newspaper offers. Sunday is usually a good choice for running classifieds ads, as many people read that section on weekends. Many newspapers offer packages which include a few other days as well.

Be sure to use an eye-catching headline. If possible, get it in bold type—you don't want your information to be lost in a sea of plain black text. Because your ad will likely be small, include the most pertinent information only. Depending on the allotted word count, try to include something that makes your business stand out, i.e. "Small, personalized group classes" or "Free consultation." You might be surprised at how much business a simple classified listing can bring.

If you can afford it, you could opt to run a display ad. A well-designed display ad will include your business name and phone number, logo, eye-catching text and, if the space is big enough, a photo. Photos really pull readers in and are worth the extra expense. Just be sure not to clutter the space with too much text.

Whichever type of ad you choose, check around for special incentives. Some publications offer a monthly or even annual rate. Test an advertisement's impact in a particular publication before committing to a long-term lease of ad space. Just keep in mind that it usually takes at least three publications of an advertisement for the general public to respond. People typically notice an ad the first time or two, then actually act on it the third time or after. Apparently repetition is a learning tool for people as well as dogs!

Telephone Directory

Another type of print ad that can be very effective is the telephone directory. Rates vary depending on which directory you choose, but most are fairly expensive. Nowadays there is usually more than one phone directory in any given area—not all pages are Yellow. Other factors that influence cost are size and placement of the ad, whether print is color or black and white, background color, photos, and size of the geographic area served. Advertising in a large city's directory will be significantly more expensive than doing so in one that services only a small, rural area. Check the area your phone directory covers, as your responses will come from all over the region served by that publication. Decide whether the fees are worth the potential clientele.

As with any other ad, keep it simple and eye-catching. I chose to place a Yellow Pages ad with a "knockout" background (the background is white instead of the usual yellow). Knockouts are an excellent and inexpensive option to make your ad stand out. I used two colors besides black in order to make certain text stand out, and highlighted a few key words by placing a starburst around them. The ad was not large enough to include a photo, but I did use my logo and with the help of the directory's art department, designed a simple, eye-catching piece that has been very effective. I did go back and forth with the art department quite a few times until I was satisfied with the results. Don't feel guilty or pushy if you end up doing the same. That's what they're paid for and besides, you'll be living with the results for a whole year. Many directories offer discounts to first-time advertisers, so be sure to check around.

Press Releases

Another way to use the power of the printed word is to issue a press release. A press release won't cost you a thing and is an excellent way to get the word out about your business. Although your goal is to advertise, a press release shouldn't sound like an advertisement. It's more like an advertorial. For example, you could present your information as, "New Dog Training Business Opens In (Your Town)." Highlight the services offered and explain how this fabulous business will benefit the community. I have included the press release I used when first introducing my business. Since I offer puppy classes, I titled another one, "Pups Get Off on the Right Paw at Puppy Kindergarten." It discussed how early socialization with other dogs and people benefits puppies. Naturally, my contact information appeared at the end of the article. Slant your article in such a way that it is likely to grab the attention of the average pet owner. Once they read about how helpful socialization, training or whatever else you include is, they'll be ready to call for more information. Contact the paper to find out specifically to whom to address the press release. (See Lisa Wilson's book for other sample press releases.)

ATT: PAT AIDEM
Fax: 661-XXX-XXXX

FOR IMMEDIATE RELEASE
Contact: Nicole Wilde (661) XXX-XXXX

Dogs Love to Learn with Gentle Guidance

Gentle Guidance, a Santa Clarita based dog training company, trains dogs and their owners. Whether in private, in-home sessions or group classes, owners learn to communicate better with their dogs, and dogs learn to listen. Both learn that training can be fun!

"Fortunately, dog training has come a long way since the old days of choke chains and harsh corrections," said Owner and Training Director Nicole Wilde. "With gentle, positive methods, dogs not only behave better, but actually enjoy the training process. Reward-based methods also strengthen the dog-owner bond. We love our dogs — so why would we train any other way?"

Wilde has worked with all types of canines (including wolves and wolf hybrids) in both training and rescue for many years. Her work as Volunteer Coordinator with the Los Angeles City Shelters, where she socialized and trained dogs and taught volunteers about dog behavior, resulted in hundreds of dogs finding loving homes.

"It's a sad fact that many of the reasons dogs are given up boil down to a lack of training," Wilde said. "So many people don't bother to train their dogs until problems have already developed. Even then, it's never too late. We give our dogs treats, toys and affection. But for a long, happy life together, training is really the best gift of all."

For additional information on Gentle Guidance's dog training services, call (661) XXX-XXXX.

Other Ways To Advertise

Flyers

A flyer contains the same basic information as your brochure, in simplified form. It is a simple statement of what you do, along with your logo, perhaps a photo, and tear-off sheets (small bits of paper than can be torn from the bottom so that the whole flyer doesn't get torn down). Tear-offs should always include your business name, rather than just your phone number. Otherwise, a week later when Joe Potential Client empties his pockets, he's likely to say "What's this?" and throw it away. (Not to mention the strife it might cause between he and Mrs. Joe!) You can easily produce a mini-flyer by printing four copies of the same design on an 8.5 x 11 page, then cutting it up. Four on a page will save you money in reproduction costs and allow you to post flyers in areas where larger ones will not easily fit.

Be creative in your flyer placement. Though bulletin boards at pet supply stores, groomers and vets are an obvious choice, they might already be covered in flyers from other trainers. What about places like laundromats, where people have nothing to do but stand around and read the bulletin board? Apartment complexes that allow pets are another excellent choice, and usually have a communal posting area. What about supermarkets? Beauty salons? The sky's the limit and the advertising is free. Go for it!

Advertising in Motion

One of the best things I ever did for my business was to get magnetic car signs. Not only do they announce my services on the way to appointments and when my Jeep is parked on the street, they work overtime wherever I drive on my time off. I always try to park where people can see the signs, even when I'm going to a movie or restaurant. I have had people strike up training-related conversations at the gas pump; call out the window from an adjacent car at a red light that they will call me about their dog; and copy down the number as they walk by. I've also had a few people call and say, "I saw your car parked at my neighbor's house. We need help, too!"

As with any advertisement, keep the design clear and simple. A wonderful local printer advised me not to crowd the signs with too much text. He was right. We used only the business name, logo, motto and phone number. (If you have a web site, you might want to include that as well.) He suggested two colors on a white background. The result is one attractive, easy-to-read sign for each door. I have since noticed signs on other vehicles that display so much information that the print is tiny and hard to read.

Since it may be a consideration for you, especially if you're female, I'd like to bring up a safety issue. When I first got car signs, I had reservations about driving around town with my phone number plastered across the side of my car. I'm female and let's face it, there are some strange folks out there. I want to reassure you, in case you have the same concerns, that so far I haven't had any problems and I don't know other trainers who have, either. Obviously, you should use caution no matter what, but I don't believe the signs are a safety risk, as long as your home address is not on them. The signs have long ago paid for themselves in training appointments. I personally think they're well worth it and besides, you can always remove them temporarily if the situation warrants it. (For training-related safety precautions, see *When Business Calls - Phone Tips*.)

Promotional Items

A great way to advertise your business is to give away promotional items imprinted with your business name, logo and contact information. Depending on the size and value of the item and on your budget, promos can be given to each client you see, used as prizes or graduation gifts in group class, as thank-yous for referrals, or as holiday gifts. As a clicker trainer, I give away clickers to all my in-home and group class clients. You can bet my information is imprinted on them! Ordering in bulk allowed me to get a great price, and it's good to know that clients will literally have my number "handy" to pass on to others.

Another promotional item I give away regularly is refrigerator magnets. I ordered mine from an online company that offers designs that are specific to pet-related businesses. The one I chose has a Cocker Spaniel in a boot that always elicits exclamations of, "How cute!" I give them to private clients and my graduating group class students. When I return to people's homes I often notice the magnet stuck on the refrigerator. Fridge magnets are one more handy way for clients to keep track of you for future training and referrals.

Other promotional items include t-shirts (a bit more expensive to produce), caps, pens, coffee mugs and more. In the *Resource* section, I have listed a few sources for imprinted clickers and refrigerator magnets. There are many companies that specialize in promotional items for businesses. Search for them online and look through their catalogs. You might get some unique ideas for promoting your business.

Other Options

Research other ways to get your name out there. Look into Money-Mailer type services, where batches of coupons are mailed to specific neighborhoods. The services are pricey but can target specific neighborhoods you want to work in. Some are mailed to residents only, while others go to businesses as well. Inquire about specifics. If you choose this option, be sure to offer a discount, i.e. "20% Off Group Classes With This Coupon!"

What about local rescue groups? Most hand out an information packet with each adoption. Your brochure should be in there! Will your local shelter allow you to place a stand with brochures at the counter? What about offering free talks at the shelter? Subjects could include Choosing a Dog, or Common Behavior Issues. Naturally, you'll have business cards and brochures on hand for prospective clients. Many rescue groups also have sections on their web site which list local trainers. Ask to be added to their listings.

There's no better advertisement than a well-trained dog. Just hanging out at the park with your dog, who is doing tricks and behaving beautifully, is sure to trigger training-related inquiries. Or, what about giving a free demonstration at the park or in front of a shop? You could speak about the importance of having a well-trained dog, or if you're a clicker trainer, dazzle 'em with a live demo of what's possible with clicker training. You're sure to pick up a few clients as you get the education out there.

Research businesses, shelters and animal-related events in your area, then brainstorm about how you can let them know about your services.

Track Your Success

Whenever you take a phone call from a potential client, ask how they were referred to you. You'll want to track how many calls you get from each advertising source. This will help you to decide whether to keep running print ads or renew your phone directory ad, know that your car signs have been noticed, or whether vets or pet stores are referring to you. Based on the feedback you get, adjust your advertising campaign so it's continually effective.

Pleased To Meet You

Now that you've got your business set up, advertising in place and handouts prepared, it's time to introduce yourself to the community.

Veterinarians

Referrals from veterinarians can account for a large percentage of your business. They are an especially valuable endorsement, as dog owners really trust their vets. Call each vet's office in your area and ask whether they have a trainer they refer to. (Or, you could check things out by stopping by in person to see whether there are brochures already on display.) When I called around, if they answered that they did not have a trainer to refer clients to, I exclaimed, "That's great, because I happen to be a dog trainer and would love to meet you!" More often than not I was able to make an appointment to visit and introduce myself. If you take this approach, be sure to be friendly and pleasant with the office staff and not just the veterinarian. After all, receptionists are at the front lines. They are the ones who will be referring people to you (or not) and answering questions when people see your brochure. In fact, I go out of my way to drop by periodically with boxes of cookies and such just to say thanks to the office staffs for the referrals. As always, there's nothing wrong with a little positive reinforcement! If you are told there is already a trainer in place, ask whether it's an exclusive arrangement. If not, they might still be open to meeting with you. At the very least, they might allow you to place your brochures in the waiting room along with the others.

So You Want To Be A Dog Trainer

Groomers and Others

Groomers are often happy to have a trainer to refer to. Their customers ask for referrals periodically, but many groomers are not aware of trainers in the area. You can easily change that. If you prefer not to cold call, bring your own dogs in for grooming, then strike up a training-related conversation. The same applies to pet supply stores. Chat with the clerk or owner the next time you go in to purchase pet supplies, and find out whether a trainer is affiliated with the store. If you plan to offer group classes, the store may be a potential venue.

Doggie daycare centers are another great source of referrals. Unless there is already a trainer on premises, they should be happy to have a good one in the community to refer to. The same goes for boarding kennels. Whether you're approaching a vet, groomer or anyone else, it never hurts to mention that your clientele are people who live in that area, and that you would be happy to refer people to them as well. (Don't do this unless you really mean it. People mention who they were referred by, and it will become obvious if you're just paying lip service.) You could end up with an arrangement that is mutually beneficial.

Stock Up

When a business agrees to let you display your brochures and/or business cards, always supply holders to put them in. Inexpensive lucite stands do nicely for brochures, and there are a variety of inexpensive cardholders. Both can be purchased at any office supply store. Place a sticker on the back of each with your business name and phone number so they can call you if the supply runs out. (This practice also stops others from appropriating your empty holders.)

Visit periodically, have a brief, pleasant chat with those who are referring to you, and be sure to keep those brochures/cards stocked. You might even want to make yourself a schedule which lists each place your cards and brochures are displayed and the last date you stocked them. This is especially helpful for keeping track if your materials are displayed at many different places around town.

When Business Calls

Telephone Tips

With your advertising in place, you'll soon be receiving phone calls inquiring about your services. Here are some tips to help handle the calls effectively:

1. The outgoing message on your answering machine should be clear, friendly and professional. Be sure your live greeting sounds the same. Once you have set business hours, let the machine pick up after hours. Even if you're a one-person company, you don't want to give the impression that you're available at all hours—it's unprofessional. You wouldn't call a doctor at home at all hours of the night, and you shouldn't expected to take off-hour calls either, unless it's an emergency. You might want to state your hours on the answering message, i.e. "Your call is very important to us. Please leave a message and your call will be returned during our business hours, 9:00 a.m. to 7:00 p.m., Monday through Saturday. We look forward to speaking with you." That way if someone calls on a Saturday night, they know not to expect a return call until Monday morning. Or, if you absolutely do not want to limit your hours at the beginning, leave an approximate time frame within which callers can expect a call back, i.e. "Your call will be returned within forty-eight hours."

2. Return phone calls promptly. My own personal goal is to return calls within three to four hours of the message being left. If you're out all day, it's a good idea to check your machine periodically for messages. I have had clients who had called other trainers and never even received a return phone call. That's not only rude, it's bad business. Be professional and return the call, even if the

69

issue is one you wouldn't normally handle. You might be able to refer them to someone else who can help, and they might well refer clients to *you* in the future, since you were the one who was so helpful.

3. Keep a phone log or spiral notebook and pen near the phone. Each time you receive a call, log the date, client's name and phone number, dog's name, breed and age, how they were referred to you, and what the call is about. Some people will want to consult with their spouse after hearing your rates and availability. Make note of that, or whatever the result of the call was. For example, "Appointment set for (date)" or, "Going on vacation, will call me next week." If you haven't logged the initial information, unless you have a photographic memory, you're faced with appearing clueless when they call back a few days or even weeks later. I have had calls where I frantically scrambled through pages of old messages as the caller was saying "My name is Denise, I called you two weeks ago..." By the time they finish I'm able to say, "Ah yes, Denise with the Bichon who has housebreaking issues." It makes clients feel good that you "remember" who they are. Writing down all the details also helps you to monitor the productivity of your print ads and other referral sources, and to keep track of how many calls resulted in appointments. If most of your calls result in appointments, great. If most don't, take a second look at your rates, phone skills or other factors that might be playing a part.

4. Potential clients will often begin a phone conversation with something like, "Hello, I'm calling to see what your rates are." Never quote your rates right away. Establish a personal connection with the client first. I usually reply with, "Sure, I'd be happy to help you with that. What breed of dog do you have?" After getting the dog's breed and age, I ask, "What type of training are you

interested in? Are you looking for basic obedience, or does your dog have a specific behavior problem?" Only after we've talked for a few minutes and I've established that I'm professional, friendly and sound like someone they'd like to train their dog, will I quote my rates. After all, if they're calling around and you simply answer with your rates right off the bat, you leave them no reason to choose you over other trainers, unless your rates are cheaper. Convince them in those few minutes that you are the one they want, regardless of rates. They might well decide to book you on the spot, rather than continuing their search. After all, they've already found the best trainer for the job!

5. While it's advantageous to draw potential clients into a conversation, once you get certain people talking about their dogs, it's difficult to get a word in edgewise. Although you need to know what the dog's behavior problem is, you don't want to spend half an hour on the phone hearing about how, "Scout came from a lovely couple who had an accidental litter, and was doing great until Aunt Fanny visited, then it all started falling apart, and Brandon, who's ten by the way, says..." It's endless. You must learn the fine art of interrupting without sounding like you're trying to cut a client short. I have used phrases like, "You know, that's fascinating and I'd love to hear more about it when I see you. Let's go ahead and set up an appointment."

6. Some people love to shop around. You will learn to recognize a phone call from the "Comparison Shopper." She typically wants lots of information, but won't commit to making an appointment. She may even tell you she's already spoken to So-and-so and their prices are lower, or they gave her some suggestions and would like your take on what they said. While there's nothing wrong with someone wanting to find the best person for the job, don't let the Comparison Shopper monopolize your time. Spend

a reasonable amount of time answering her queries, then offer to set up an appointment. If she declines, ask her to call back when she's ready to do so.

7. Closely related to the Comparison Shopper is the "Information Mooch." This guy is not really looking to make an appointment with you or anyone else, ever. He figures that as a professional trainer, you should be willing to answer his questions over the phone, free of charge, for as long as he likes. There is nothing wrong with giving someone a quick, simple solution to a problem that doesn't require an in-home appointment; just don't let the Information Mooch suck you into a long, involved conversation about his dog's issues without making an appointment.

8. When you quote your rates, be specific about the fees and what they cover. For example, let's say your rate for in-home training is fifty dollars an hour, and the first appointment usually lasts an hour and a half. Don't just say, "My rates are fifty dollars an hour" and assume that clients will do the math. Once you've completed a ninety-minute session, they might be surprised to hear that the total is seventy-five dollars, not fifty. Many people hear that "fifty dollars" and tune out the rest, which could lead clients to believe the entire session will cost them fifty dollars regardless of the length of the session. It's far better to lay it all out for them at the start. For example, "My rate is fifty dollars per hour. The first session usually lasts an hour and a half, so that would be seventy-five dollars for the first session. Sessions after that last one hour only, so they would be fifty dollars."

If you sell packages of sessions, let the client know up front how many they would be expected to purchase and how much they can potentially save by doing so. If you do non-packaged sessions, make it clear there is no further obligation after the first session.

A word about negotiating your rates: *don't*. If someone tells me they are interested but the rate I've given them for ninety minutes is a bit high, I might say, "I understand that money is an issue. What I can do is keep the first session to an hour so it would only cost you ___. Would that be helpful?" What I will *not* do is drop or negotiate my rates. It is one thing to decide in advance to give a discount rate to someone who has adopted from a rescue or shelter, or has some extenuating circumstance. However, letting someone talk you down from your original quote is not only unprofessional, but I promise you, will earn you a client who is not going to value your advice as much, and will forever be trying to get more out of you at less cost to them. Don't haggle.

Note: It's a strange phenomenon in American culture that many people feel the things we pay for are valuable, while those given away free are not. Be careful about where you place your charity. Telling someone you'll work with their friend because she's really strapped for cash right now and you feel badly for the dog may lead to you spending lots of time and effort and the friend not really valuing your advice. After all, it was free. It's great to offer free classes at shelters or to work with rescue dogs gratis, but beware of offering free training where it's not likely to be taken seriously or appreciated.

9. Do not make guarantees. While it's tempting to tell a client that you know their problem is absolutely solvable, no matter how strongly you feel it is, don't guarantee it. Dogs are living beings and there is no way anyone can guarantee their behavior one hundred percent. When asked if you can fix a behavior problem, you could certainly reply with something along the lines of, "I've dealt with this same issue many times and have not yet found a case where I couldn't put it right." That's different than saying, "I absolutely guarantee I will fix your dog's behavior

problem." The former inspires confidence. The latter could inspire a lawsuit.

10. Try not to feel pressured into taking a case, whether it's a behavior issue you're not comfortable with, someone is not willing to pay your full fee, or any other reason. People will call you with all sorts of stories, wanting you to do things that are totally outside the scope of your business. Just the other day, a woman phoned me regarding her Bichon's barking problem. She lived in an apartment, was gone all day, and the poor dog emitted a high-pitched bark for hours on end. The neighbors were complaining. I told her I would be happy to set up an appointment with her. She informed me that she'd already spent a lot of money on another trainer who was not able to solve the problem, and if she didn't fix the problem within the next three days, the dog was to be debarked. Now, at this point I would probably counsel you, my soon-to-be-training friend, that you are running a business and there's not much you can do if the woman doesn't want to pay you. I will admit to you, though, that I ended up on the phone with her for another half hour giving free advice, as the thought of that little dog being debarked horrified me. What I'm saying here is, while it's good to have compassion and to do what you can, try not to feel pressured into doing things you don't want to or really shouldn't do on a regular basis. As always, if it's an area such as aggression that you are not comfortable dealing with, refer the case to another trainer.

11. After establishing that the person on the phone is a potential client, i.e. their dog's needs fit in with the services that you offer, and your rates and availability are acceptable, it's time to "ask for the sale." While I am in no way a fan of the hard sell (in fact it really turns me off), you must be a bit of a salesperson. Instead of asking, "Would you like to make an appointment?" (which

leaves them the option of choosing not to) say, "When would you like an appointment? Are you available mid-week?" You're not being pushy, you're being efficient. If someone really sounds unsure, I don't push them. Some might disagree with this, believing you shouldn't take anything but yes for an answer, but I have found that pushing someone to make the appointment when they're not entirely committed only leads to a cancellation as the day approaches. Do what's comfortable for you. As you go along, you'll develop your own style.

12. Try to schedule appointments when the whole family can attend. It is more productive as far as clarity and compliance for spouses and children to hear instructions directly from you, the professional, than second-hand from each other. Plus, you can gain valuable information by observing each family member's interactions with the dog. Having children present can be especially useful, since kids often blurt out useful information that parents wouldn't necessarily offer!

13. If for any reason you get an uneasy feeling about someone on the phone, ask a *lot* of questions. Every now and then, I get weird vibes on the phone from a male potential client. When that happens, I ask a *lot* more questions than I normally would, such as where the dog came from, how long they've had it, why they picked that breed and more. My initial hesitancy is usually dispelled. If it's not, I find some excuse to turn down the appointment. (If you are stuck, tell them someone is at your door and you'll call them back. That will buy you some time.) Listen to your gut feeling and don't ever take an appointment you feel wary about just because you need the business. It's not worth it.

Safety Precautions

- Always have your cell phone easily accessible.

- If you are doing a private, in-home session, let someone know where you will be. I keep a wipe-off board on the wall and note the name, address and phone number for my husband, just in case.

- Keep your vehicle in good working order. Depending on what area you live in, breaking down can be dangerous, not to mention detrimental to your business. Keeping up on oil changes, tune-ups and general maintenance is mandatory and potentially tax-deductible.

- Ironically, I had a new client just the other day who insprired me to add another point here. When I arrived for our appointment the man was in his driveway, searching for something in the back seat of his car. After I introduced myself, he said he could not find his checkbook to pay me for the session. He suggested, "Why don't we drive to the ATM machine so I can get you some cash." While it turns out the guy was harmless (and no, I did not go with him and he finally found the checkbook), this brings to mind another safety tip: Never get in a car with a client you don't know, for any reason!

Trainer Etiquette

Just as a friendly, knowledgeable manner on the phone will impress clients, a professional in-person presentation will continue the good impression.

Promptness

Wear a watch. Always arrive at your in-home appointment or group class on time. While being delayed in traffic is understandable, if you're going to be more than five minutes late, call to let your in-home client know. If it's a group class, apologize when you arrive. If you have more than one consecutive in-home appointment scheduled, try to end each session at the prescribed time so you can keep on schedule. One session that runs twenty minutes over can throw off the rest of your day.

Appearance

In the business of dog training, no one expects you to show up in a three-piece suit. However, your appearance and personal hygiene are the first things people notice. Let's take two trainers, Mr. A and Ms. B. Mr. A is roughly forty pounds overweight. That's no crime, except that the way his dirty T-shirt rides up over his belly, you'd think he was proud of the fact. His jeans have tears at the knees and his hair is perfect...that is, for an off-Broadway production of *Grease*. As Mr. A leans forward to shake the client's hand, it becomes obvious that he prefers his cheeseburgers loaded with onions. What an impression, and the training hasn't even begun! Ms. B, on the other hand, arrives wearing a clean T-shirt and jeans. Her hair is washed and tied back neatly. Her breath is fresh. She appears friendly, alert and ready to work. Which trainer would *you* want at your home? Don't be lazy. First impressions say it all. (Personally, I'm so paranoid about bad breath that I always pop a breath mint before walking into a client's home!)

Keeping Time

If you find the big hand inching past the hour mark on a scheduled hour-long in-home appointment, call the client's attention to it. No one wants to be charged for extra time they didn't realize had passed. Simply say, "I'd love to show you that exercise we discussed, but I want to let you know that we will end up running past the hour. If we go another extra half hour the fee will be ___ total. Is that acceptable?" Always give the client the choice.

Be Polite

Of course you know it's a good idea to be polite to clients, whether in a group setting or one-on-one. But trust me, there will be clients even Miss Manners would be tempted to strangle (though she'd probably use a freshly pressed tie). Though the majority of clients you deal with will be pleasant, inevitably there will be be some who are argumentative, rude, ignorant, annoying, or any combination of the above. Remain polite. Do not allow yourself to be drawn into an argument. After all, you're the professional.

Read up on dealing with difficult people. In any customer service industry the same client types exist, and some wonderful books have been written on the subject. (See *Resources* for two that are specifically geared toward dog trainers.) Keep your cool. Some argumentative clients, when faced with your cool composure, will calm down themselves. Just as you wouldn't respond to an aggressive dog with force, don't do so with a client and risk escalating the confrontation. Remember your positive reinforcement techniques! Sometimes just reiterating what the client says is helpful: "I can understand how frustrating it must be to come home and find urine on the carpet. So, instead of continuing to rub the dog's nose in it, why don't we talk about crate training and management. That way you won't have to deal with this stress any longer." Of course, this is said in a calm, soothing voice. Calm and soothing is helpful when responding to stressed and unbalanced. Call a friend after the appointment or group class and vent if you need to.

Of course, if the rudeness involves something like responding to one phone call after another during your in-home appointment, you are perfectly within your rights to suggest letting the machine pick up the calls. After all, you want the client to get the most out of the session (and you not to tear out your hair). If the problems have two legs and are throwing tantrums and constantly interrupting, you might suggest the parent give them something else to do like coloring or playing a video game in the other room. (After all, you'd give a puppy who was chewing on the carpet something else to do—dog-training and kid-training isn't all that different.)

Another aspect of being polite is not interrupting while someone speaks. Many of us are already thinking of the next question we want to ask while the client is answering the current one. As time is always an issue, it's hard not to jump in before they are finished. You may find this especially challenging if, like me, you are a high-energy, keep-on-track sort of person. If necessary, jot your next question down so you can concentrate on what the client is saying and not feel that you have to interrupt them. You might just catch a piece of information that is crucial to the case.

While waiting for the client to finish speaking is polite, some clients will launch into lengthy stories about their dog and even unrelated topics. You will have to reel them in. When you sense an opening, gently guide the conversation back to the subject at hand. You can always say something like, "You know, that's really interesting and I'd love to hear all about it, but we only have another half hour and I want to make sure we get to all the topics we wanted to cover today." This is especially important during a group class, as one person can easily monopolize your time and throw the entire class off track.

The majority of in-home clients will offer to shake your hand at the door. While in human language this clearly conveys, "Pleased to meet you," to a dog who is protective of its owner, it might mean something else entirely. In fact, the dog might take your reaching toward their owner as a serious threat, and you could get bitten. I'm not suggesting you never shake anyone's hand, but that you be well aware of the dog's body language before doing so. There is nothing wrong with saying, "Please don't think me rude, but I would just as soon not shake your hand, as I can see it might make your dog uncomfortable." Rather than being offended, they will probably be impressed that you are so observant of their dog's body language.

Be Honest

If a client asks a question you don't know the answer to, it's perfectly okay to say so. While you are expected to know certain things, if you get stumped, just respond with something like, "That's a good question, and I'd like to give you a great answer, so I'm going to consult with one of my colleagues and get back to you." Of course, if the question is totally out of your area, say so and if possible, refer them to a source that might have the answer. If the question involves a medical issue, just say you're not qualified to give veterinary advice, and refer them to their veterinarian. If it's something simple like, "Do you know any good remedies for dry skin?" and you do, go ahead and answer. But answering a question like, "Do you think I should put my dog on Rimadyl for his hip dysplasia?" can get you in trouble. You are not qualified to give veterinary advice and could end up being sued if something goes wrong. Even if you recommend a natural remedy, suggest that the client clear it with their veterinarian first.

If You've Got Nothing Nice To Say...

Turns out your mother was right. If you don't have anything nice to say, don't say anything at all. It's awfully tempting, when a client mentions another trainer who you know to be an awful trainer, abusive to dogs, offensive to people, or whatever, to jump right in and roast that person along with them. Don't do it. Speaking poorly of others only makes *you* look bad and is definitely unprofessional. Besides, what does it accomplish? If a question is put to you where you feel you absolutely have to respond, you could always say, "I don't like to speak poorly of other trainers" and leave it at that. That says it all without you having to explain further.

If someone asks about a local veterinarian whom you think is awful, instead of saying, "Oh, I've heard terrible things about him!" respond with, "I don't have any personal experience with him, but here's the name of someone I do know and think is wonderful." There is a trainer in my area who used to be referred out by a local veterinarian. This trainer spoke poorly of the vet to a lot of his clients. (Not terribly bright, considering the clients were referred by the vet in the first place.) Word got back to the vet. He is currently suing the trainer for slander. So you see, it really does pay to be pleasant and to keep your tongue in check. Besides, the people who spend the most time putting others down are usually insecure themselves. Rise above it and concentrate on improving your own skills and reputation.

Your Toolbox

In the "Member Profile" section of the APDT newsletter, one of the questions asked of the profilee is, "What's in your toolbox?" No, it doesn't refer to screwdrivers and wrenches, but rather, the Training Toolbox: collars, leashes, clickers, toys, treats and anything else the trainer keeps on hand for training sessions. Your toolbox should include items that are proactive, in that they keep dogs busy so they're not getting into trouble in the first place. It should also contain management tools, educational materials and stuff that's just plain fun. You will find your toolbox expanding over time, along with your knowledge and experience. So without further ado, to borrow a line from Julie Andrews, "These are a few of my favorite things." I use many of these with my own dogs. They have certainly helped a lot of my clients and their canine companions. If you can't find these items at your local pet supply store, try the *Resources* section, or one of the many suppliers who advertise through catalogs or online.

Interactive Food Toys

1.The Kong ™

I often joke that I should be working for the Kong Company. I so love their product that I recommend it to just about every client. The hard rubber Kong ball is shaped like a snowman and comes in a range of sizes and two densities (standard red and tougher black). The wonderful thing about it, besides that it bounces unpredictably, is that there is a small hole on top and a large one on the bottom, which can be stuffed with treats. (Stay away from the tiny sizes, as there's not enough room inside to stuff anything.) Dogs will spend a considerable amount of time and effort attempting to get the treats out. You can even freeze or microwave food treats in a Kong! My own dogs, who range between 80 and 120 pounds each, will spend upwards of thirty minutes excavating a well-packed Kong; and trust me, it's not easy to find something that my steel-jawed fur-kids won't shred and ingest immediately.

Sometimes I feed my dogs' meals in their Kongs. I mix a little bit of wet food with their usual dry kibble, stuff the balls, and don't hear a peep from them for a while. My mealtime-Kong-stuffing technique is on a handout I give to clients, along with other recipes and ideas. Clients should be encouraged to enrich their dogs' lives in any way possible. So why present a boring bowl of kibble when their dog can have something to work on that is both stimulating and time-consuming? There are some great ideas for Kong-stuffing on the company's web site (see *Resources*). The tips are also available by request in the form of a booklet called "Recipe for the Perfect Dog," which you can distribute to your in-home clients and group class students. (There is also a great web site on Kong stuffing by a trainer named Mary Strauss at http://members.home.net/mstraus/treatref.html#kong.)

Kongs can be especially helpful for dogs who are left alone for long periods or suffer from separation issues. A yummy Kong presented just as Mom leaves could help to alleviate anxiety. Kongs are also helpful for dogs who must be crated for a period of time. They are a wonderful way to keep dogs busy when company is over or the owners simply want to relax and have some time to themselves. I have one client who calls the Kong a "Puppy Pacifier." She's right! There are plenty of things a puppy won't get into while she's intent on getting the treasure out of that ball, and as all puppy parents know, not having to watch a puppy every moment is a beautiful thing.

At in-home training sessions, I often stuff the tiny hole of the Kong with a chewy treat, so clients can see first-hand how intensely their dog tries to get it out and how busy it keeps them. (This also gives me a chance to speak with the client uninterrupted.) It's as though the dog goes into a Zen-like trance, and I have only stuffed the tiny hole! Most clients run out to buy a Kong after the session, and their dogs couldn't be happier. I always have a Kong or two on hand for group class as well. It's amazing how far one rubber ball stuffed with peanut butter can go to calm a dog who is barking or stressed out, thereby keeping the peace in class.

Ah, the power of the Kong!

2. Buster Cube™

Here we have another great, keep-'em-busy tool. The Buster Cube is a hard plastic "dice" with a hole on one side and four chambers inside. It's easy to fill, which is something clients really like. Just pour kibble or small, dry treats into the hole, then shake to distribute the goodies throughout the chambers. It's that simple. The dog then paws and rolls the cube around to make the treats fall out. Again, why give dogs their meal in a dish when they can spend all that extra time and energy working for it? Besides, it's great mental stimulation. My own dogs love it when they get their meals this way, and your clients will love the fact that their dogs, especially the super-active breeds, are getting all that energy out in a productive way.

Note: This food cube may be inappropriate for large, strong dogs whose goal in life is to disembowel anything they are presented with. The long tube which ends in the hole where the kibble goes in can be removed by especially tenacious dogs. If you're not sure whether your dog is a disembowler like my Mojo boy, be sure to supervise the first time your dog tries it.

3. Havaball™

Since my own fur-kid is intent on dismembering the Buster Cube, I recently tried out a new product called the Havaball. This octagonal-shaped ball is a cross between the Kong and the Buster Cube. It's made of hard rubber, with side strips meant to encourage dental health. There is a hole on one side which can be filled with dry treats such as kibble or cookies; it dispenses the goodies easily when rolled around. (The treats fall out more easily than with the cube, so it might not keep dogs busy as long—then again, the thing stays in one piece with disembowlers like Mojo.) The toy comes in different sizes for different-sized dogs. My dogs love theirs, and clients appreciate the ease with which it can be filled.

Gentle Leader™

In my opinion, the Gentle Leader is one of the best dog-related inventions ever. This head halter is similar to the Halti, which has been on the market for years, but the design affords a more customized fit. It consists of two conjoined yet separately adjustable nylon strips, one of which goes over the dog's muzzle, and the other, around the head. (The muzzle strip does not restrict the dog's ability to bark, drink water or anything else he could normally do.) It buckles (or snaps, they come both ways) behind the dog's ears, rather than around the neck. The Gentle Leader is often described as "power steering" for dogs. It's true. Mojo weighs 120 pounds, which is more than I weigh soaking wet. He's well trained, but if he sees a cat all bets are off. You can imagine what walking Mojo would be like on a regular collar! The Gentle Leader allows me enough control enough to gradually teach him that cats are not hors d'oeuvres.

Many dogs are not taken for walks because it's such an ordeal for their humans. Those dogs often become understimulated and underexercised, and various behavior problems can result. The Gentle Leader can make all the difference for those dogs, breaking the cycle and improving the quality of life for them and their humans. Many trainers also believe that the Gentle Leader has a calming effect on dogs who are fearful, and can help to change the attitude of aggressive dogs.

It is important to become completely familiar with the Gentle Leader before using it with clients' dogs. Practice fitting it properly and walking your own dogs with it first. Premier, the company that manufactures the Gentle Leader, has a video available which shows how to properly fit and use it. There is also a booklet which comes with each Gentle Leader that you can give to clients. Not only do I recommend Gentle Leaders, I sell them as well. This affords me a little extra income and saves clients the trouble of going to the store. It also allows me to be sure the fit is correct and to give the client and dog some supervised practice. If you wish to sell Gentle Leaders or any other Premier products, set up an account with the company so you can purchase them at wholesale prices. (See *Resources*.)

Some dogs do not like the feel of any head halter at first. I explain to clients that it is like getting used to wearing glasses or a bra. At first it is uncomfortable, and is all you can think about. After a while you forget it's even there. If it's a couple I'm working with, I usually turn to the male client at this point and say, "You remember your first bra, don't you?" (Okay, I have a weird sense of humor. Lucky for me they always laugh.) While some dogs resist at first, most adjust quickly, especially if the Gentle Leader is paired with treats and/or walks. The client may also condition the dog gradually, before ever going for a walk. Have them put the Gentle Leader on the dog, feed treats/pet/praise for thirty seconds, then remove it and ignore the dog. They should do this two to three times a day for a week. *Note: Premier recently decided to make their 3/8" muzzle loop (usually used for shorter-muzzled breeds) standard on all Gentle Leaders. They are thinner than those shown below, so should cause even less resistance.*

Martingale Collars

The same company that makes Gentle Leaders (Premier—see *Resources*) also offers martingale-style collars, sold under the name The Premier™ collar. Martingales look similar to the regular nylon buckle collars we're all familiar with, but have an extra strip of nylon with a ring attached, which makes them operate like a limited slip collar. The leash attaches to the ring on the extra strip. When pulled, it brings two rings on the main collar together so it tightens but does not choke the dog. Martingales give more control than regular collars, and are especially helpful for dogs who tend to slip out of their collars, like narrow-headed sighthound breeds.

Clickers

Clicker training is a non-coercive, super-effective, fun way to train dogs. Though I don't use clickers for every training situation, you can bet there is always a large supply in my toolbox.

A clicker is similar to those tin crickets that were popular as party favors when we were kids. Modern clickers consist of a metal tab inside a rectangular plastic shell. When depressed, the metal tab makes a clicking sound. The basis of clicker training is that the click is a marker that tells the dog the exact moment he is doing what we want. Each click is followed by a treat. (Why else would a dog care about earning a click?) For example, we might lure a dog into a down position, clicking only when his body is flat on the ground. Once the dog is performing the desired behavior consistently, we simply give the behavior a name, i.e. add a verbal cue (i.e. "Down") just before the behavior happens, so the dog associates the two. The dog will eventually respond to the verbal cue, and the use of the clicker and treats can be phased out.

Clicker training is often used in conjunction with food luring, but it can also be used to shape or "capture" behaviors. Shaping refers to rewarding successive approximations of a behavior (breaking it down into small pieces and rewarding and building on them). Capturing a behavior means clicking and treating when the dog happens to do something on his own, i.e. yawns. If clicked often enough, the dog will start to offer the behavior. Clicker training teaches dogs to think for themselves, and is mentally stimulating to both dog and trainer.

If you are used to traditional training where commands are issued, dogs are manipulated into position and then praised, clicker training may seem odd to you at first. It's worth getting your mind around these strange-seeming concepts. Owners are constantly amazed at how quickly their dogs learn and how well they focus with clicker training and to be honest, it's just plain fun to train this way! I have listed some great clicker training books and videos in the *Resources* section, along with sources to purchase clickers. My own clickers have my company name, logo and phone number imprinted on them. Yours should too! I give clickers to every private client I use them with.

Treats

It's a good idea to have a few different types of treats with you at training sessions. After all, treat-training is difficult if the dog doesn't like your treats! If you get stuck you could always ask the client whether they have something on hand the dog likes, but it's always best to be prepared.

Everyone has their own favorite training treat. Mine is Dick Van Patten's Natural Balance dog food rolls. Natural Balance comes in a sausage-like roll, has healthy ingredients and smells almost like beef jerky. Mmm. In fact, I had a client once who left the roll in her refrigerator when she and her family went on vacation. They came back to find their cleaning person had been making sandwiches with it! For training treats, slice the roll up, then dice each coin-shaped slice into small, pea-sized squares. (Any training treats should be roughly pea-sized and easily chewable.)

Other popular training treats include string cheese and hot dogs cut into coin-size slices. If you don't like the greasiness of hot dogs, nuke them in the microwave for thirty seconds, then cool before using.

Assess-A-Hand

Trainer Sue Sternberg, who does incredible work with shelter dogs across the country, is responsible for a wonderful invention called the Assess-A-Hand. This simple but brilliant tool consists of a wooden dowel covered by foam and a man's shirtsleeve, with a plastic hand at the end. Although it doesn't look exactly like a human arm, it is realistic enough that some dogs will most definitely take exception to it reaching for their food. I can not emphasize enough how valuable the Assess-A-Hand is when testing for resource guarding. I used it once to help temperament-test a Chow mix. As the dog hovered over his food, I moved the hand slowly from behind into his peripheral vision, toward the food. The dog not only snapped at it, he bit it repeatedly, moving up the hand toward me! I have to admit that I and the other people standing nearby jumped about five feet in the air. Not only was I thankful to have been using the Assess-A-Hand, I was also glad I had purchased the extra-long "Rottweiler length" version! The Assess-A-Hand is also useful for getting leashes on fearful shelter dogs and for testing for stranger-approach/aggression (to gauge whether the dog would actually bite if someone came up and petted him). See *Resources* for ordering information.

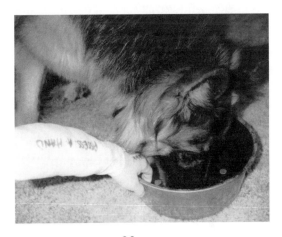

93

Tethers

A tether is a short length (usually four feet) of plastic-coated wire cable with metal clips on both ends. One end clips to the dog's collar and the other, to an eyebolt fastened to the wall. Alternately, a tether can be made by looping a short leash around a banister or heavy furniture leg, which is helpful for those who don't want to put eyehooks into their walls. (It might be necessary to spray the leash with a taste deterrent.) The main purpose of a tether is to keep a dog contained in one area.

A tether is useful in many situations. It can be used to teach a dog to settle down while its humans relax; to manage multiple dogs who are enjoying chew toys, to prevent fighting over them; and, a tether can be helpful for housebreaking. Dogs will not soil in their own little area. A tether drastically reduces that area. If an owner is occupied, a destructive or non-housebroken dog could be tethered so as to keep out of trouble. See the April 2001 issue of the *Whole Dog Journal* (listed in *Resources*) for instructions on how to make your own tethers.

Note: Tethers should only be used when owners are present, rather than to keep the dog immobile when alone. A dog bed should be provided, along with a stuffed Kong or other chewy.

Taste Deterrents

Taste deterrents come in sprays and creams, and are used to prevent dogs from chewing on things we'd prefer they didn't. They are typically used on furniture, but can be applied to many items. The most popular brand is Grannick's Bitter Apple. This classic standby is effective with a large percentage of dogs. There is a small constituency, however, who consider it a delicacy and will lick it enthusiastically wherever it is sprayed. Do you have to ask? Yes, Mojo loves it. Since no brand will deter every dog out there anyway, it's good to have a few on hand. Pet supply stores usually stock at least two or three brands. If you keep a few in your toolbox, you can perform a taste test with client's dogs to see which ones elicit that "yuck" response, thus saving the client money by not having them buy the wrong thing, and impressing them with how prepared and effective you are.

Knowledge

That may seem like a strange, intangible thing to include in your toolbox, but it is possibly the most valuable thing you have to offer (along with a sense of humor!). All the gadgets, treats and toys in the world won't mean a thing unless you understand how to effectively use them. The more solutions you have to a problem, the better. Let's say your client has a dog who is generally stressed and fearful. What's in your toolbox besides behavior modification techniques? Are you familiar with herbal remedies? Bach Flowers? Holistic remedies? What about Ttouch (a form of massage that is extremely effective on animals)? The more you know, the more you can offer in terms of possible solutions.

Knowledge of local resources is also important. What if the dog's behavior issue would be best addressed by burning off some energy during the day, rather than being confined to the yard alone? Are you familiar with any local doggie daycare centers? What about a competent petsitter/dogwalker? Perhaps a local agility class dog and owner could attend would help. You don't have to learn about everything at once, but do keep your ears and mind open constantly. Become a repository of information. It might not seem immediately useful, but there will be a time when it will come in handy.

Other things to keep in your toolbox include leashes, collars, long-lines, toys, target sticks (for clicker training), balls, bandages and other first aid supplies (just in case!), books and handouts. You may have noticed there are no choke chains or electric shock collars in my toolbox. Personally, I do not use them. For an informative online article on choke chains and electric shock collars, point your web browser to www.sfspca.org/gifs/pdf_dogrights/choke.pdf.

Preparation For In-Home Sessions

Phone Screening

We've already discussed general business practices for taking incoming calls. Here are some specific questions to include in your phone screening:

1. Dog's breed, gender and age. These three bits of information can give you a heads-up on possible reasons for behavior issues. For example, Terrier breeds are known diggers; older dogs will be more set in their ways than younger ones.

2. Is the dog spay/neutered? This can be an important factor when it comes to issues such as dog-dog aggression and male marking.

3. Does the dog have any medical problems? Just as people act differently when they are in pain, so do dogs. Although it's not the first thing to look for in every situation, in cases that involve the sudden onset of aggressive behavior, a medical problem could well be the cause. On a less dramatic note, you will want to know about medical issues so you don't, for example, recommend a strenuous exercise program for a dog with hip dysplasia.

4. Are there other animals in the home? Note breed/age/gender.

5. Are there other people/children in the home? Age of children? Having young children in the home can affect the severity of a behavior issue. For example, it's one thing for adults to live with a dog who guards his food, but quite another when a small child is involved. Knowing whether there are kids involved will allow you to plan your behavior modification program accordingly.

97

6. Is the client interested in obedience training, or in need of help with behavior issues?
   a. If obedience, has the dog had any previous training? What does he already know?
   b. If behavioral, what is the main issue? How long has it been going on? Get a brief description.

7. Are there other behavior issues? Sometimes this question helps to bring up things the client would not otherwise have thought to mention. For example, the call might have been prompted by the dog chewing on the table leg, but when you ask about other problems, they mention that he also lunges at people on walks.

8. Does the dog live indoors with the family or in the back yard?

9. Has the dog ever bitten or attempted to bite another animal or a person?

While some of these questions could be skipped or glossed over during the phone call in favor of addressing them in person, that last one is not negotiable. *Be sure to ask about aggression even if it seems totally out of context with the issue the client is calling about.* I once had a client call with the complaint that his dog, a sweet Dalmatian/Australian Shepherd mix, had chewed numerous garden hoses and was destroying the back yard. I walked in to find Cerebus, the three-headed beast that guards the gates of hell! This enormous 120-pound Pit Bull/Mastiff mix (my best guess) had the largest head and bulging eyes I have ever seen on a dog. That the eyes pointed outward in different directions didn't help any! I had met the family outside and followed them into the house. They had no problem walking past Cerebus, but apparently I was not to get past that entryway! As he snarled at me, saliva flying, it was apparent that not only was he not happy to see me, but his biggest problem did not involve garden hoses. I used all the proper body language and "calming signals" I could think of. This dog looked at me and said in no uncertain terms, "#$*% you *and* your calming signals!" Now, obviously this boy had some major aggression issues, a fact that could have been mentioned on the phone. It certainly taught me a lesson about remembering to ask whether a dog has ever threatened anyone! (I stayed for the session but to be honest, at the time I probably should have referred it to another trainer. Remember, there is nothing wrong with admitting that you're uncomfortable with a case, or that you don't have all the answers. Besides, that way you get to keep your pride and all your body parts.)

Should you decide to take the appointment, get the correct spelling of the client's name (and the dog's name), address with directions if necessary, home phone and alternate phone number (i.e., cell phone or work number). Also, remember to ask how they were referred to you. If the appointment you set is not until a week or two later, you might want to call the client the evening before to confirm/remind them.

Keeping Track

So you've spoken on the phone, jotted down some notes, and now you're ready to go—or are you? Where will this data you have so diligently recorded be saved? How will you record further pertinent information when you interview the client in person? It helps to have a Client Sheet already set up. This form will not only help to keep track of important information, but will give you a place to record what you do at each session so you know where to pick up the next time.

I have included a copy of my own client record sheet as an example. I keep my basic form on the computer and modify it as needed. You will develop one that works best for you. You might want to add a ratings section, where you could circle Fair, Good or Excellent (or a scale of one to five) so you remember how you felt about the session. You could even develop a code of notations such as DC for Difficult Client, EC for Excellent Client and so forth (I recommend codes rather than writing the phrases out just in case you ever leave your notebook at a client's home!) Client Sheets can be three-hole punched and kept in a loose-leaf binder. Just be sure to periodically remove inactive clients to keep current and organized. You could also transfer client information to your computer, making sure to back up the data regularly.

Name: _____   Date: _____

Address: _____   Dog's Name: _____

_____   Breed: _____

Phone: _____   Age/Sex: _____

Ref. by: _____   Spay/Neut.? _____

Other Pets in Household: _____

Other People in Household: _____

Veterinarian: _____

Medical Problems: _____

Has dog ever bitten or injured a person or animal? If yes, describe:

_____

_____

Where did dog come from/How long together: _____

_____Housebroken? _____ Crate trained? _____

Indoor/outdoor? _____ Where does dog sleep? _____

Brand of Food: _____ Fed how many times a day? _____

Has dog had any previous training? If so, describe (include what cues he knows):

_____

_____

Daily Exercise _____

Reason for Consultation: _____

_____

Notes: _____

_____

_____

101

Scheduling

When it comes to scheduling in-home appointments, try to stick with a work load and time frame you are comfortable with. While you are somewhat at the mercy of clients' availability, if you've decided that Sunday is your day to spend with your family, don't take a Sunday appointment just because a client suggests it would be more convenient. It's awfully tempting, especially when you first start out, to bend over backwards to accommodate clients. If you compromise too much, however, you will end up with appointments at odd hours, working at times you are not at your best. Strive for a comfortable balance.

Once your business starts picking up, scheduling and limits will become even more important. Some trainers are comfortable doing two to three in-home appointments daily, while others can handle five. You will develop your own preferences as you go, along with a feel for how much time to leave between appointments for travel time, etc. If you schedule a heavy day or two with multiple sessions, try to make the next day light or completely free. Of course, some trainers prefer to spread appointments out more evenly. If, for example, you are at your most energetic and happy to work in the morning, but are lethargic by 4:00 p.m., you might want to spread your appointments out over as many mornings as possible, then have the rest of your days free. It's really a personal decision.

However you set up your schedule, be sure to take care of your health and get enough rest. If you have a few appointments in a row, bring along a cooler with snacks like string cheese or yogurt to keep your hunger down and blood sugar steady. Coolers also come in handy for keeping extra dog treats fresh. Exercise or do other stress-relieving activities you enjoy. Take short vacations now and then to recharge your batteries. Every job, no matter how enjoyable, carries the potential for burnout. Dog training can contribute not only to physical stress but to mental stress as well. Setting guidelines and limits from the beginning, sticking with them and taking good care of your mind and body, will go a long way toward ensuring a long and rewarding career.

The Appointment

The time arrives for your appointment. Naturally, you are prompt, presentable and ready for work. Now what? You have just a few seconds to make that first impression, so be friendly and professional. Smile and introduce yourself. As you do so, take notice of the dog's behavior. (If the case involves human-directed aggression, you should have previously arranged to have the dog outside or otherwise managed for your arrival.) You can obtain vital information by simply observing the dog as you speak with the owner, both at the door and as you sit and chat. Note the owner's interactions with the dog as well.

Spend whatever time is necessary to get all the pertinent details regarding the issues mentioned during the phone screening. You will also notice things in the environment that will prompt you to ask further questions. A good trainer is part detective. Often the piece of information that solves a behavioral puzzle is something you must ferret out, rather than relying on the client to offer it. (If you love puzzle-solving, you will probably enjoy working with behavior issues.)

Once you've chatted with the client, you should have a solid idea of what the important issues are; or, if the focus is on obedience training, what needs to be taught. Always establish from the start what the client's goal is. If, for example, the dog is chewing the garden hose, is the client's goal solely to have the dog stop chewing the hose? Or is there a larger overall goal, i.e. to ultimately bring the dog indoors to be part of the family, so it won't be bored and therefore chewing hoses? It's important to know what the *client* wants. What *you* think is best for the dog may differ. That is one of the challenges of this profession. All you can do is give the client the facts, along with your expert opinion, and hope they go along with it. It's tough not to blurt out things like, "Why did you get a dog if it's going to be in the back yard alone all day?" Unfortunately, that would not only be unprofessional, it would alienate the client. Remember that saying about catching more flies with honey than with vinegar? It's true. For example, you will get further with clients by nicely pointing out why spanking the dog isn't really effective, and by offering alternatives, than you will by blaming or berating them. And in the end, you'll be helping the dog.

As far as the specifics of actually working with dogs, many of the books in the *Resources* section provide specific instruction on basic obedience and behavior issues. There is no way to cover that vast amount of information in these pages. Regardless of which issues are involved, here are ten tips that will help you in any in-home training session:

1. *Try to minimize distractions.* Recommend to the client in advance that they let the answering machine pick up calls during the session. If there are other pets in the household, suggest they be placed in another room with a yummy chew toy while training takes place. Young children should be provided with an activity like coloring, homework or watching a video. Otherwise you might find yourself interrupted constantly, which makes training difficult if not impossible.

2. *Don't assume that the information the client provides is accurate.* It might well be their perception of the way things are, but you will get more information by keeping your eyes and ears open and observing the dog's behavior and client-dog interaction. Note what the client says, but don't take it as gospel. The dog will give you the real story.

3. *Be patient with the dog.* Let fearful dogs come to you; don't pressure or coerce them. Constantly monitor the dog's reaction to your actions and don't push training to the point where the dog is getting stressed or frustrated. It's okay to take short breaks if necessary. Let the dog's behavior dictate how much you cover during a session.

4. *Be patient with the owners.* After all, at least half of dog training is training the owners. Try not to get frustrated when someone doesn't understand or can't perform an exercise. Break things into small steps for them, just as you would for the dog. As trainer extraordinaire Bob Bailey says, "Training is a mechanical skill." When someone is first trying to juggle a clicker, treats and leash, it's difficult! Be supportive and make it easier for them if necessary. Remind them that when they first learned to drive, it was hard to concentrate on all those things at once. Like driving, after some practice, training becomes fluent and natural. And remember, it's just as important to reinforce owners when they get something right as it is with the dogs. People need encouragement and positive feedback too!

It's good practice for you as a dog trainer to learn a new skill once in a while. I recently enrolled in a bellydancing class. Trust me, coordinating all those isolated movements is not easy, and I found myself with a whole new empathy for those clicker-leash-treat juggling clients!

5. *Stay focused.* Refrain from telling long, involved stories about your own dogs or your training experiences. While a brief mention of something personal and relevant might be helpful, a long, drawn-out account of your personal adventures might well cause

the client to wonder why they're paying by the hour to listen to it. Be sure to cover the main issues you came to address. If you feel there are other issues that need attention say so, and schedule another session if necessary.

6. *Show, don't tell.* If you expect the client to carry out a program, don't just hand them a protocol and expect them to follow it. Step by step, show them exactly what you want them to do with the dog, then have them practice it. Instructions on paper don't always translate the way they're meant and besides, most people learn better by actually doing things hands-on. Walking the client and dog through procedures allows you to give feedback and guidance, and should the dog not react in the expected way, to modify the exercise as needed.

7. *Offer a few possible solutions to the problem.* Together with the client, decide on one that is feasible. Even the best solutions are worthless if they don't fit in with the client's lifestyle, capabilities or commitment to carry them out. Make programs simple and realistic, with specific instructions on what to do and how and when to progress to the next level. For behavior modification issues, you may need to give specific instructions each week as you go along, rather than laying out the whole program at the start. That way the client won't get overwhelmed, can stay on track, and you can modify the program as you go along.

8. *Don't take failures personally.* It's inevitable that at some point, something you're attempting will not work. Hey, sometimes the dogs just haven't read the right training books. If it happens, simply take a moment to analyze the situation, then come up with another way of tackling the problem. You might need to break the behavior down into smaller steps for the dog to understand.

Or, you could switch to another approach altogether. The ability to revise your program on the fly is part of the art of being a good trainer and will develop as you go along. You will also find that programs sometimes fail because owners don't comply with your instructions. It does not mean you've failed. Know that you have done the best you could. Sometimes things are out of our hands.

9. *Just say "No."* If it becomes clear that the problem is not what was represented to you on the phone and is not something you are comfortable working with, say so. There is nothing wrong with bowing out gracefully and referring the problem to another trainer.

10. *Reality check, please!* It is inevitable that you will come across owners who have unrealistic expectations. It is sometimes difficult for novice trainers (and even more experienced ones) to tell owners that what they want from the dog is simply not going to happen. After all, we all want to please the owner and feel that we are good enough trainers to get the dog to do what they'd like. However, it is important to develop a feel for where the line is between high expectations and unreality, and a knack for telling owners so in a nice way. Remember, most owners really do love and want what's best for their dogs, but unfortunately, some do not have a firm grasp of canine behavior. Expecting a dog to urinate in a specific spot in the yard is realistic, so long as the owner is willing to leash the dog and lead him to that spot repeatedly at the start. Expecting an unneutered male dog to stop marking over the spot where another dog keeps urinating is unrealistic. Whenever possible, strive to reach a compromise whereby the owner still gets what they want and the dog is set up to succeed. If that's not possible, tell the owner in a nice way that what they want is simply unrealistic to expect of *any* dog.

So You Want To Be A Dog Trainer

The Wrap-Up

So your session's gone well and now it's time to depart. Leave the client with business cards and any handouts that apply. Be sure they understand how to proceed with the training program and if necessary, schedule another appointment. If another appointment is not warranted, you could ask the client to call you in a week or two to let you know how things are progressing. Or, say you'll call them. Follow-up calls are a good way to gauge the success of the programs you prescribe and to help with any snags that may have arisen. They also offer an opportunity to make another appointment if necessary. And, following up shows your concern for how dog and owner are doing.

Be sure to record session notes in your notebook or hand-held dictaphone for later transcription. It is too easy to forget exactly what was accomplished if you wait too long.

A Few Last Tips Regarding In-Home Training

While these tips don't apply to the actual visit, they are important for any trainer who does in-home training:

- Well-meaning acquaintances or clients will often have a friend who is interested in training. They may ask that you give them a call. *Don't do it.* People who are not motivated enough to call you themselves have a low likelihood of following through with a training program. Thank the person for the referral and ask them to pass your number along.

- If you get to an appointment but the client is nowhere to be found, wait fifteen minutes. Traffic jams and other inevitable delays happen. If the client still has not shown, leave a pleasant note on the door stating that you were there for the appointment, you hope everything is okay, and you will call them to reschedule. You could even have the notes pre-printed. As annoyed as you might be, don't leave an offensive note. It will get you nowhere and who knows, there might have been a real emergency. Besides, even if you have a cancellation clause in your contract, it will be difficult to collect the fee if the client isn't speaking to you. When you call back to reschedule, if there is a cancellation fee involved, remind the client that it will be due at the next appointment.

- See aggression cases as the first appointment of your day, or whenever you are most alert and thinking clearly. Do *not* see aggression cases if you have not slept the night before or are otherwise "out of it." It is better to reschedule than to make a serious misjudgment.

- Sooner or later, you will come across a client who just won't let you go. You've helped them with their initial concerns and maybe a few others; the dog is doing fabulously. The client, however, has become attached to your weekly visits. There can be many reasons for this, from a lack of confidence that they can continue the training on their own, to loneliness, to simply enjoying your company. The ethical thing to do is to let the client know you have completed the training that was agreed upon, and they are fully capable of continuing it on their own. Should they say they simply feel better going on a few more weeks with your assistance, or they'd like to find other things to work on, great. So long as the client is still getting something out of the training sessions and you are willing to continue, go for it.

Preparation For Group Class

There are various types of group classes. The most common is basic obedience for adult dogs. Some trainers also offer intermediate and advanced classes. For puppies, there are "kindergarten" groups which focus on socialization, puppy issues and some basic obedience. Other classes specifically offer clicker training. A clicker training class usually includes basic obedience, along with other clicker-friendly options such as targeting (teaching dogs to touch a target with nose or paw) and shaping behaviors. A more specialized type of class is a "growl class," which focuses on dogs who are reactive/aggressive with other dogs. Although growl classes are becoming more popular, they are not something a novice instructor should attempt. A great option for a class that a novice/intermediate instructor could teach, however, is a tricks class. This type of class can be taught with or without clickers. Naturally, I vote for with! A tricks class can be one of the most fun groups you will ever teach. People have a light-hearted attitude while teaching tricks; they and the dogs end up having a great time while they learn. Strive to infuse even your basic obedience classes with that light-hearted, fun atmosphere. After all, those obedience maneuvers are all just tricks to the dogs!

Where?

The first thing you will need is a training space. Some trainers are lucky enough to have their own indoor facility. While you probably won't start out that way, if there is space available within a pet supply store, for example, ask whether it can be rented by the hour. Other indoor spaces to check into are school gymnasiums, groomer's shops, veterinary offices, veterans halls, dance or martial arts studios or community recreation rooms. Outdoor options include parks, parking lots (i.e. outside a pet supply store or church), school grounds, or someone's back yard. If you plan to teach a puppy class, you will need a safe space where the pups are not in danger of contracting disease. For this reason, a public park is not the best place to hold a puppy class.

How Many?

Once you have a space reserved, you'll still have a few decisions to make. First, how many dogs will be allowed in each class? The number will depend on how much space you have to work in, whether you work alone or with assistants, what you're comfortable with and what's financially feasible. Although there is obviously more money to be made with larger classes, there is also less personal attention given (unless you have assistants), which can be frustrating to both you and the owners. You will probably start out by teaching on your own, so keep your class size manageable. Since I prefer to work alone, my classes are limited to six dogs. That way I can give enough personal attention to each and keep track of what everyone is doing throughout the class. You could even, as previously mentioned, offer very small classes, marketing them as exclusive, "Semi-Private" groups.

How Much?

Once you decide how many dogs you will accept, set your fees. Call around to see what the going rate is in your area. Be sure to calculate your fees based on the minimum number of dogs you will accept in class so that if you don't have a full group, you won't end up selling yourself short.

When?

Schedule your classes at times which are convenient for the general public. Weekday evenings are popular, as are weekend mornings, late afternoons or early evenings. In the summertime, avoid giving classes in the heat of the day; it's uncomfortable and potentially dangerous for both dogs and people. (If you can't avoid the heat, suggest that people bring water for their dogs and themselves, and sunscreen.) If you're working indoors you won't have to worry about the weather or having enough light. Set evening classes late enough to give people time to get home from work, but not so late that people won't be motivated to come. Evening classes usually start around 7:00-7:30 p.m.

How Long?

A basic obedience course for adult dogs usually lasts somewhere between six and ten weeks. Classes meet once a week, for one hour. Some trainers, myself included, prefer to do the first class without dogs present. That way, people can pay attention without worrying about what their dogs are doing, and everyone can do some practice exercises. I know other trainers who feel clients get more out of it if the dogs are there from the beginning. If you do the first session without dogs, you might want to extend your class one session longer. If you are doing a specialized class such as a tricks class, you could opt for a less traditional structure, such as three or four two-hour sessions.

Advertising

Once you've considered all of these factors, it's time to advertise. If you are offering classes through a Parks Department, they will probably advertise for you. If your classes are to be held at a vet's office or through a pet supply store, you probably will leave a sign-up sheet on the premises, then call people to give them more information. You might also post flyers around town and advertise in local publications. Be sure to emphasize what's special about your class. For example, let people know that it's a clicker training class, or that they'll be playing games, and that it's a fun and effective way for them and their dogs to learn.

Phone Screening

When you phone prospective students, be sure to review the class date and time, fees and what the class will cover. Inform them of any specific policies; for example, the age at which children are allowed to attend (ages eight and over are welcome in my classes) and at what age and vaccination status dogs are eligible. Then be sure to ask a very important question: *Has their dog ever bitten or attempted to bite another dog or person?* Ask this specifically, rather than, "Is your dog aggressive?" Some people have a very different definition of "aggressive" than you or I. It's crucial for you to have this information, as it is quite unpleasant for class members (and you!) to be surprised by a dog-aggressive or people-aggressive dog in their midst. A seriously aggressive dog is not only an unfair imposition on your students and their dogs, but is a potential liability. Suggest private behavior modification sessions instead.

Note: While a seriously dog-aggressive dog has no place in an average group class, if you're comfortable with it and have the space, you could accept dogs who are simply "reactive" with other dogs. In other words, they might bark and lunge at other dogs, but it is usually fear-based. It's their way of saying, "Stay away from me, you big scary thing!" Most reactive dogs I have accepted into class were either afraid or were bullies, technically more "dog-obnoxious" than dog-aggressive. If you choose to accept dog-reactive dogs in your classes, don't allow more than one (or two at the most) in any given class. Inform owners at the start that the dog is not seriously aggressive and is no threat to their dogs, but it would be appreciated if everyone could help by letting him keep his distance. Have the dog and owner work away from the other dogs and slowly move in as progress is made. The owner should be instructed not to jerk or yell at their dog when the dog reacts, but to simply get the dog's attention and walk away in a large circle with the dog at their side to refocus them if necessary. In almost all the cases I have encountered, the reactive dog was able to work in much closer to the other dogs by the end of the last session. And, even if they were too stressed to completely absorb the training, if they simply learned to be more comfortable around other dogs, it was worthwhile.

Form Letters/Contracts

Once you've established that the dog is a good candidate for class, get the owner's address and send them a form letter. The letter should cover where and when the class will be held, the fee, what to bring (i.e. treats, vaccination records) and class rules. I have included a sample letter. Along with the letter, include a contract which releases you and the provider of your teaching space from liability, should a mishap occur. Ask that the contract be signed and returned with payment in order to guarantee their spot in class. Getting payment in advance is an invaluable practice. That way you know for certain how many people will be attending, and can avoid giving a class for only a few people or having too many to manage.

So You Want To Be A Dog Trainer

This is the body of the form letter I send out. It would normally be on letterhead with the date, full address, salutation and signature:

Congratulations on choosing to train your puppy using Gentle Guidance's dog-friendly, people-friendly, positive methods!

The puppy class you are enrolling in will provide plenty of playtime/ socialization with other pups. We will discuss solutions to common problems such as nipping, chewing, jumping up on people and more. Your pup will also get an introduction to: sitting when asked, lying down, and coming when called. You will learn about canine behavior and body language, and how dogs think and learn.

Please bring: *Location*: *ABC Veterinary Clinic*
- Current vaccination records   *832 Hemingway Ave.*
- Your pup, wearing a plain collar   *Yourtown*
(Please, no choke chains or retractable leashes)   *800-555-0655*
- Food treats: Bring treats cut into pea-size pieces, i.e. hot dogs, cheese, freeze-dried liver, Natural Balance roll. Or, if your pup has weight or health issues, use your puppy's regular kibble (dry food) - put it in a sealed plastic bag the night before with chicken or hot dog. In the morning, remove the chicken/hot dog. The kibble will have absorbed the yummy chicken/hot dog flavor.

Please enter the training area with your pup on leash, and do not approach other pups. Although there are no aggressive dogs in class, a supervised, safe introduction is always best. All family members are welcome, including children eight years of age and over.

Please sign and return the enclosed Training Services Agreement, along with payment ($60). This will guarantee your spot in class. Class starts on Monday, August 20th at 7:30 p.m. and runs for four Mondays. Please save this letter for class location, date and time. I will phone you before the start date to touch base and answer any last-minute questions. I look forward to having you and Sadie in class!

DOG TRAINING SERVICES AGREEMENT

Dog's Name:			Owner's Name:
Breed:			Home Phone:
Age:	Sex:	Weight:	Work/Cell Phone:
Spay/Neutered?			Address:
Vaccinations current?			City/State/Zip:
Vet's Name:			Vet's Phone:

Training Fee:	$60.00	Start Date: Mon. Aug. 20, 2001
Duration:	4 weeks	Location: ABC VeterinaryClinic
Time:	7:30 - 8:30	832 HemingwayAvenue, Yourtown/800-555-0655

First class is no dogs, people only. Please bring vaccination records.
Classes are filled on a first-come, first-served basis. A spot will not be held until payment is received along with signed Training Agreement. These items must be received prior to commencement of first class.

SERVICES PROVIDED: Classes are taught by Nicole Wilde ("Trainer"), a professional dog trainer. Classes are limited to 6 dogs so personal attention may be given to each dog-handler team. Trainer, at her discretion, may refuse entry to a pet which is not healthy, is aggressive or does not seem suitable for the services provided.

PAYMENT: Payment is due prior to the start of training. No refunds will be given.

REMOVAL FROM TRAINING: Trainer, at her sole discretion, may remove a pet from class if a hazard or threat of any nature to any other animal or person is present. No refund will be given under such circumstances.

DANGER: Owner agrees to indemnify and hold ABC Vet and all Staff ("Location") and Trainer harmless from all liability for any loss, damage or injury to persons, animals or property arising from or related to Owner's pet. Owner agrees that Location and/or Trainer shall not be liable for loss or damage to animal for any reason unless said loss or damage was a direct result of Location or Trainer's negligence.

ARBITRATION: Any controversy between the parties involving any of the terms, covenants, or conditions of this Agreement shall be submitted to arbitration in Los Angeles County, California, on the request of any party, and shall comply with and be governed by the provisions of the American Arbitration Association. All decisions shall be final and binding. In any dispute between the parties, whether or not resulting in litigation, the party substantially prevailing shall be entitled to recover from the other party all reasonable costs, including without limitation, attorney's fees.

SIGNATURE/DATE: _____ ("Owner") _____ ("Trainer")

119

The Group Class

What's the Plan?

Regardless of which type of class you choose to teach, you will need a lesson plan which outlines what you will cover during each lesson. Make a list of the behaviors you want to teach during the course. For example, a basic obedience class usually covers Sit, Down (lie down), Heel (or the less formal "loose-leash walking"), Come (also called the "Recall") and Stay. Many trainers also teach Attention exercises. After all, if you don't have the dog's attention, you're not going to get much of a response to anything else! In addition, some trainers include "Leave It," a.k.a. "That thing you were about to put in your mouth—don't even think about it!" and "Settle" (lie down and relax). These are just the basics. You will fill in your syllabus with other topics, games and exercises related to the behaviors being taught.

The First Class

The first session is an appropriate time to go over class rules. Discuss protocol for dog-dog interactions, asking questions, and anything else you think is important. The first session is also the time to check vaccination records, collars (for correct fit and type) and to collect any contracts or monies due.

In my adult group class, there is no time specifically set aside for canine socialization, but if the dogs are friendly and the owners would like, the dogs may mingle on-leash before or after class. That's important for owners to know before the dogs ever arrive on the scene. In my own classes it's not a problem since the first class is for people only. If you have dogs present at the first class, you could outline dog interaction rules in your form letter and remind owners of them by telephone before class starts. Naturally, you will have to remind students of the rules as you go along.

As far as questions during class, if they pertain to what we're working on and are not specific to just one person, I'm happy to address them. After all, there are no stupid questions, and someone else is probably wondering the same thing. More individualized questions can be raised during the fifteen minute pre-class setup time, or for fifteen minutes afterward. If you prefer not to answer questions before or after class, you could ask students to phone you with questions during the week or, you could designate the last ten minutes of your class as a question and answer period. (Trainer Janine Pierce has a ten-minute brainstorming session at the end of each class. A student poses a training or behavior question, then Janine and the students offer answers. This is an excellent way for students to stay involved; and, many students come up with excellent, creative solutions!)

It's standard procedure for everyone to introduce themselves and their dog at the first class. Remember to introduce yourself as well. In my classes, owners are asked to give their name, dog's name, breed and age, and to share one thing they really like about their dog. That last bit is very revealing. You will often get a foreshadowing of things to come when someone answers, "I can't really think of anything" or, "Oh, there are so many things I couldn't possibly list them," or even, "I like that she matches my couch." (And yes, I have actually heard that last one!)

The first class is also the perfect time (especially if dogs are not present) to explain the basic principles of dog training and how they apply to what you'll be doing. This includes how dogs think and learn, the advantages of positive methods over punishment, how and when to reinforce behaviors and more. This is all stated briefly, without scientific jargon. For example, if you want your students to progress from giving treats each time their dog sits to treating every couple of times, say so, instead of announcing that they are "moving from a continuous reinforcement schedule to one of random ratio, intermittent reinforcement." Otherwise, you'll end up with a room full of glazed expressions, and I don't mean the dogs.

If dogs are not present and you're teaching clicker training, the first class is an excellent time to let owners practice with the clicker. Owners can break into pairs where one plays the dog and one the owner; the owner clicks and treats for simple behaviors like the dog making eye contact. (People really get into this game. Some even start barking and scratching!) Or, students can do exercises that will improve their timing, such as you dropping a ball and asking them to click before it hits the ground. Many clicker trainers play the "Training Game" during the first class. One student is sent from the room, while the others decide on a simple task he/she must perform, such as picking up a specific object. The student returns. Each time she moves in the direction that will ultimately accomplish the task, the other students click. The game teaches owners the valuable skill of shaping a behavior by breaking it down into small steps. (For a more in-depth description of this game, see *Resources* for Karen Pryor's *Don't Shoot the Dog*.) Have I mentioned how much fun everyone has playing this game? It's a major laugh-fest!

Note: While having people only present the first night of class lends itself to clicker training practice, many trainers choose to have the dogs there from the very first class. If you do so, be sure to tell owners to reward any time their dog is calm. Rewarding calm really cuts down on first-night chaos.

Lesson Progression

When planning your courses, keep in mind that there should be a natural progression of behaviors. For example, the first thing I teach in Basic Obedience class is Attention. Once dogs are more focused on owners, the owners can move on to teaching Sit. Down is taught after Sit, because (in my courses) Down is taught from a sitting position. Keep in mind that some behaviors, like Sit and Down, are fairly quick to teach. Others, like getting a solid Recall, a long Stay or walking nicely on leash are more of a process. So although Sit and Down are introduced almost immediately, you will probably want to begin working on other behaviors early in the curriculum as well. The goal is to introduce each behavior, then expand on it. Get students to practice each behavior at home with no distractions at first, then move to different areas of the house, then outdoors with no distractions, and finally "proof" it with distractions in and out of class.

You will find that you are constantly modifying your lesson plans depending on the specific dogs and people in that class, the pace they can handle, how much time questions take up, etc. Try to stick with the overall plan but don't get stressed if you find yourself straying from it, or not getting around to minor things you wanted to include. That's the nature of the beast. You will become adept at planning as you go, so it all comes together regardless of setbacks.

Following is an example of what a single behavior might look like throughout your course. In this example, Down-Stay is introduced in Class Three. We are assuming here that the dogs have already learned Sit and Down.

Keep in mind this is not an explanation of exactly how a behavior is taught, but rather, how it progresses:

Class Three: Dogs are in down position. Owners stand right next to dogs. Dogs are rewarded for 3-5 second down-stays. If a dog can't manage three seconds, owner begins with whatever dog can do. Owners are instructed on how to work with dogs on duration at home, adding time very gradually without moving away from dog. Goal is to do a one minute down-stay.

Class Four: Assuming dogs can now down-stay with owner next to them for a minute, owners take one step away. Dogs down-stay for ten seconds (or if not able, whatever dog is capable of). Instruct owners on how to build distance gradually, i.e. each time they add a step away, to go back to a ten-second stay (or less if necessary) and build up. Goal is to get one to three steps away from dog during home practice.

Class Five: Owners to introduce small distractions at close range while dog remains in down-stay, i.e. walking around dog, bending to tie shoelace, doing a jumping-jack, bouncing a ball or squeaking a toy. Owners continue to build duration of stay at a distance.

Class Six: More distractions are introduced. While owner remains close to dog, another dog/owner team walks by at a distance. While owner is a few steps away from dog, another person walks slowly in-between, or comes up to shake owner's hand.

Class Seven: While dog down-stays with owner at a distance, an adult student or child runs past. In another exercise, half the students practice recalls while the other half keep their dogs in down-stays.

Class Eight: Graduation! Games are played that include down-stay skills. For example, all dogs down-stay in a line, at a distance from each other. One dog-owner team weaves through, with dog in heel position. They place themselves at the end of the line and the next dog/owner team goes. This can be done as a relay race with owners broken up into two teams, with penalties for dogs breaking down-stays. Don't forget prizes for the winning team!

This plan is only one example. You will find what works best for you by trying different things and modifying them over and over. Keep in mind that the goal is to build on each behavior as the class progresses, so that by the last class, the dogs can perform the behaviors even with distractions. No one expects a novice class to end up with dogs who are "bomb-proof" (won't react no matter what the distraction), but aim for the best results the dogs and owners in your class are capable of.

Homework

Along with lesson plans, you will need to prepare homework assignments. Keep them short and simple. Review how to train the behavior and give helpful tips and specifics on how to proceed. For example, rather than saying, "Practice Sit this week," you might suggest that once the dog has mastered Sit, the owner ask the dog to sit before meals and having the leash put on for walks; practice with the dog sitting by the owner's side, rather than facing them; and with the owner sitting, then cueing the dog to sit. Some trainers hand out a checklist to help owners progress in an effective manner. Homeworks are also an appropriate place to include any lecture material that is important but would have taken up valuable class time (and probably not have been fully absorbed). Lecture material might include information about behavior issues, leadership, health concerns, etcetera.

Graduation

It is great fun to have a group graduation at the last class. After all, everyone has been training diligently for the past few months. They deserve it! Graduation Day is the time to point out how far the dogs and owners have come and to let them show off. It's fun to play games that incorporate what's been learned, complete with prizes. Graduation certificates may be handed out, along with a small parting gift for each student/dog team. The atmosphere should be one of light-hearted celebration.

There is a wonderful game called *My Dog Can Do That* (see *Resources*), which is a hoot to play at graduation. The game consists of a deck of cards, each of which has a task the owner/ dog team must perform to advance. The cards are conveniently broken down into beginner and more advanced tasks, so you can use those which are appropriate to your group. I can not express the laughter and rollicking good times my students have had playing it. It is so satisfying to see people draw a card, say "No way, my dog won't be able to do this," then watch as their dog *does* do it. They inevitably find their dogs capable of much more than they thought! Other fun games to play at graduation include relay races and Musical Chairs. (For Musical Chairs, play as you would for people, but don't let owners take a seat until their dog is sitting. Mats or hula hoops may be substituted for the *dogs* to sit on/in.) Terry Ryan's booklets and Roy Hunter's book (see *Resources/Miscellaneous Books*) offer more great game ideas.

Graduation certificates can be printed on certificate paper (available at any office supply store) using your home computer. Gold foil stickers are also available, which add a nice touch. Print programs are available which include templates for certificates, or you can make your own template using a word processing program. Students really enjoy being presented with graduation certificates. I have known quite a few who have framed and hung them on their wall.

Along with the certificate, it's nice to have a small giveaway item. I really like *Bark Bars*, which are cookies shaped like cats and postmen. They come in cute bags, are cost-effective, get a laugh, and are healthy for the dogs. (See *Resources*.) Many trainers make their own gift bags, which might include dog treats, clickers, toys, or discount coupons on products or classes. Be creative!

Saying Goodbye

Be sure to mention any upcoming classes you have scheduled, as many students will want to go on to the next level. If you don't offer next-level classes, try to have a referral ready to someone in your area who does. If you do in-home training, now is the time to remind owners they can always contact you for individual help. Be sure everyone has your business card. If you have personalized fridge magnets or other promotional items, distribute them. That way students always have your number handy, and you stay in their minds for future training and referrals.

Puppy Kindergarten

While many of the same considerations apply regardless of which type of class you offer, there are some that are specific to puppy class, a.k.a. Puppy Kindergarten:

Safety First

When it comes to young pups, safety must be your first priority. Owners have a legitimate concern about their puppy contracting parvo or distemper by walking or playing in an area where infected dogs have been. For that reason, most puppy classes are held indoors, in an area which has been thoroughly disinfected beforehand. Other safety considerations include making sure flooring surfaces are such that pups won't slide and injure themselves, and that there are no sharp objects or obstacles pups could run into.

Many veterinarians recommend puppies not be exposed to other dogs until all vaccinations are complete (usually at sixteen weeks, when the rabies vaccination is given). However, many trainers offer classes to pups as young as ten weeks of age, so long as they have had at least two rounds of vaccinations and are in good health. The period of development during which socialization has the optimum effect ends at approximately twelve weeks of age. That does not mean pups can not be socialized after that, but that it is most effective to do so during that period. It is up to you and whoever owns the space you train in as to what age to accept pups in class, but remember this: *More dogs lose their lives as a result of not having been socialized and trained early on (i.e., are given up for behavioral reasons and end up euthanized), than from contracting a disease.*

If you choose to accept very young pups, be sure to establish a maximum age as well so you don't end up with very young pups being overwhelmed by much older/larger ones. My own class is open to pups three to five months of age who have had at least two rounds of vaccinations and are in good health. (The three month figure is based on what the vet whose space I teach in is comfortable with.) Some trainers offer classes for pups ten weeks to four months of age. As far as actual physical size, some trainers prefer to accept only dogs of approximately the same size, so as to avoid potential injury during play. Some accept any pup of the appropriate age, then separate dogs by size by using a puppy pen for smaller breeds. My own personal belief is that having a mix of sizes and interactions is preferable. Small dogs should learn to play nicely with large dogs and vice versa. Of course, supervision should be constant to ensure that none of the pups are getting hurt or overwhelmed.

Once people have signed up for your class, learn a bit about each breed that is enrolled. Familiarize yourself with what each was originally bred for and what their tendencies are, so you can relate it to training. For example, someone who has a Terrier might have more of an issue with digging than someone with, say, a Shiba Inu. When the owner of the Australian Shepherd asks why she chases their son when he walks away from the rest of the family, you could explain about the herding instinct. At the first class, when people introduce themselves and their pup, you could offer comments on each breed, i.e., "Did you know that well-bred Pit Bulls are very stable and are actually excellent with children? They really have gotten a bad rap!"

Curriculum

While a Puppy Kindergarten class may offer some basic obedience training, it should also address puppy-specific issues and include plenty of time for socialization with other pups and people. I love it when kids attend my puppy class with their parents, as it gives the pups positive exposure to kids as well as adults.

My own puppy classes are limited as far as obedience exercises. I teach Attention, Sit, Down, an introduction to the Recall, Leave It and Settle (lay quietly). Due to limited space, however, loose leash walking is not included. You might want to include it in your class, as well as the ever-helpful, "Go To Your Bed." Behavioral issues you might want to address include housebreaking/crate training, jumping up, nipping/mouthiness, barking and other attention-seeking behaviors, door-darting, digging and preventing separation anxiety. Other possible subjects to cover in class or via handouts include establishing leadership, which chew toys are appropriate, periods of canine social development, and things that are potentially hazardous to puppies.

I don't hand out homework sheets in my puppy class, but you certainly could. I do give out a wonderful booklet by Gail Pivar and Leslie Nelson called *Taking Care of Puppy Business.* (See *Resources.*) It promotes setting puppies up to succeed by using good management and positive training, and has sections on housebreaking, crate training, playbiting/mouthing, first aid, the importance of exercise and more. It even lists plants and household substances that can be toxic to canines. The book is inexpensive, especially if you buy in bulk, and provides students with valuable information. (If you are concerned about the cost, you could always raise your enrollment fee by a few dollars to cover it.)

Decide on the length of your course and plan your curriculum accordingly. Most puppy classes run six to eight sessions. Mine is somewhat unusual in that it runs only four sessions, which focus mainly on socialization, handling exercises, puppy issues and some introductory obedience exercises. Owners then have the option of enrolling the pups in a basic obedience class. Some trainers offer a brief puppy class like mine, calling it Puppy One, then offer a Puppy Two class, which covers whatever basic obedience the pups haven't yet learned. You could also offer a standard six-to-eight week puppy class that includes all the basic obedience work, then let them graduate to an intermediate class.

Be sure to touch base with owners before the first class begins. Remind them to bring vaccination records, treats and anything else that is required. Many trainers also ask owners to bring a mat or bed for their pup. This gives the pup its own personal space in class and is useful in teaching "Go To Your Bed." Some trainers ask owners to bring their pup's favorite toy, to keep them occupied when necessary. Try out different strategies and do what works best for you.

Rules for Playtime

It is especially important in puppy class to discuss rules for interaction, both human and canine. Will dogs be on leash or off? Are pups allowed to sniff and check each other out at any time during class? What if someone's pup lunges at another? Should the owners pet other pups? In my own classes, owners are instructed to keep pups on leash, close to them, until instructed otherwise. When pups are introduced, which usually happens in pairs, leashes are kept slack so the pups don't become defensive. When I feel it's safe, owners are instructed to drop the leashes. (Leashes are left trailing so the dogs can be grabbed quickly if necessary. Some trainers prefer to unclip leashes so as not to tangle.) Owners get plenty of time to pet and play with all the pups during games like "Pass the Puppy" (more on that in a moment), but they are instructed not to pet (and thereby reward) a pup who wanders over and jumps up on them.

As the pups play, I comment on what their body language is saying, point out stress signals, and urge owners to do the same. Many owners believe the growls and barks that accompany play are a sign of aggression. They are quite relieved when you point out that these signals are completely normal in the course of play. Of course, when a pup displays truly inappropriate play behavior, you should break up the interaction. In my experience, by the end of the fourth class, all five dogs are playing off-leash together and the owners are comfortable with it.

Here are some suggested rules of interaction for Puppy Kindergarten:

1. No dogs off-leash unless you give the word.

2. When dogs are off-leash, if any owner is uncomfortable with what's going on, they may yell, "Grab your dogs!" and everyone must calmly get their own dog. This gives owners a sense of control over what's going on.

3. No dog should ever become cornered. After all, any dog could become defensive and bite in that situation. "Being cornered" does not apply only to physical corners, but could mean the pup is hiding behind the sitting owner's legs.

4. If two dogs are playing and one seems to be getting overwhelmed, pull the "top dog" off gently and restrain him for a

few seconds. Observe whether the other dog runs away and stays there, or darts back in to continue the game. Very often what we feel is unfair or overwhelming is normal play for dogs.

5. If you sense play between two pups is escalating into something more serious, separate them for a few moments. If necessary, have everyone grab their dogs and take a break. This is a good time to employ the "Settle" (relax and settle down).

Fearful Pups

In many puppy classes, there is at least one pup who hides behind its owners' legs, wishing to be elsewhere. This is perfectly understandable behavior in a pup who has never been exposed to others. In my own classes, every one of those pups has improved as the class went on. In fact, some turned into real social butterflies! The trick to getting fearful pups more comfortable is two-fold. One is to let them progress at their own pace, not forcing any interactions upon them. Be sure that none of the other pups runs at or corners them, or even interacts with them if they aren't ready. If necessary, bring a card table and stand it on its side, so the fearful dog has something to hide behind. (This is also helpful for dogs who bark at other dogs.)

The trickier part involves training the humans not to unwittingly reward the pup's fear. Many dog-parents, particularly those with small breeds, tend to pick the pup up and coo soothingly at the first sign of distress. The trouble is, the dog never learns to stand on its own four feet. Even those who don't pick the pup up often reward with a reinforcing, coddling tone of voice whenever the dog shows fear. It's not that we want the dog to be traumatized; just the opposite. We want the dog to see that the pack leader, the human, is obviously not worried by what's going on, so there is no need for them to be, either. There is a huge difference between saying in a sing-song, jovial voice, "Silly, that's just another dog. Go play!" and soothing the pup with an overbearing, "Oh, my poor Poopsie, did that dog scare you?" Pups take their cues from their humans. You may have to remind owners repeatedly during the course not to reward fear. They may, however, reward their pup with soft praise for interacting with the other pups. Fearful pups *will* improve in your classes when allowed to move at their own pace with their owners acting appropriately.

Let's Play a Game!

Games that teach pups and give them confidence should be played throughout Puppy Kindergarten. "Pass the Puppy," where everyone gets a chance to handle each dog, teaches pups to accept human handling and is invaluable for future vet and groomer visits. When the signal is given, pups are passed to the person next to them. If the pups have already learned Sit or Down, everyone takes a turn at getting each pup to perform the behaviors. This often results in gales of laughter and comments such as, "Can we keep this one instead?" Depending on the pups' comfort levels, owners could also play at petting each pup in various ways. For example, they could tug lightly at the tail or ears, or pat the pups palm-down over the head with a pat-pat-pat motion. After all, it's inevitable that a child or even an adult will approach the pup that way, and it's best for them to get used to it now. The fact that each tug or pat is followed up with a treat gets pups to actually enjoy the contact.

I usually play Pass the Puppy at the second class, when the dogs are beginning to relax. Don't force fearful pups to be passed around if it will make them too uncomfortable. Instead, have the owner bring the pup on leash to meet each person. If even that is too overwhelming for the pup, have them sit the game out. Just watching all the commotion is plenty. You will be surprised at how much fun this game is for pups and people, and will no doubt come up with your own twists on it.

Another fun Puppy Kindergarten activity is Dressup Day, where owners don strange hats, dark sunglasses, fake noses, costumes, uniforms and anything else they'd like, and wear them for the duration of the lesson. (You could ask them to come dressed for the occasion, or have an assortment of hats, glasses, etc. on hand.) Anything goes! Kids really get into this game. The more serious purpose is that pups get familiar with these potentially scary things in a fun way. Owners could even wear the strange accessories while playing Pass the Puppy.

There is an endless variety of games that can be played in a puppy class. You could place a pile of socks and T-shirts in the middle of the room, then have a race to see who can dress their pup in them fastest. If you have the space, you could have owners play Hide and Seek with their pups (one at a time), each owner hiding and then calling their pup. Hide and seek is great for teaching pups to keep an eye on and check in with their owner, and is good practice for the recall.

Other Puppy K Activities

In addition to fun and games, Puppy Kindergarten should include handling exercises, with specific instructions on how to handle pups, especially around the feet, ears and mouth. There should be restraint exercises as well, which mimic what a veterinarian or groomer would do. Owners should be instructed not only on how to hold or restrain their pup, but to hold firmly if the pup squirms, then praise gently and release when he relaxes. Massage is another important thing to include. Daily massage is a wonderful way for owners to bond with their pups and can alert them to physical abnormalities they might have missed otherwise, such as cysts or tender spots.

You should also provide "foreign objects" for pups to get used to, such as a child's expandable tunnel, a plastic ladder laid on the ground, a low A-frame, a cardboard carton to climb through, or any other weird thing you can think of. Once pups have been introduced to each object, you can even combine the objects into a makeshift agility course. Interacting with new things boosts pups' confidence. It also gives you an opportunity to coach owners on their own reactions when their pup displays fear at encountering unfamiliar objects.

Puppy Graduation

Although it's certainly not mandatory, I love ending Puppy Kindergarten with a graduation ceremony. Owners are so proud of their little ones. Graduation night puts a smile on everyone's face and ends the course on a high note. I play a puppy version of the "My Dog Can Do That" card game, which is always fun. You might choose to play Musical Chairs, or have a contest such as which pup can do the most Sits (or Downs, or Puppy Pushups, which are Sit-Down-Sits) in one minute. Or, have a contest for the longest eye contact with owner, or even something silly, like the best tail wag. Certificates and prizes are handed out, along with a list of great dog training books, business cards and promotional fridge magnets.

At the end of puppy class, it is important to give owners information about what to do next. If you don't offer a basic obedience class to move on to, refer them to someone who does.

Stress the importance of continuing to socialize the pups and incorporating the learned obedience exercises into their daily routines. Tell owners that just because their pups have become comfortable around other dogs, that does not mean they will stay that way. A pup who goes to class but has no continued exposure to other dogs will, over time, become "desocialized" and all that hard work will be out the window. Suggest they get together with others in the class for play dates, as well as meeting new dogs outside of those they've known in class. And, give yourself a pat on the back for getting those pups and owners off to a great start.

Group Class Tips

Whether you're teaching classes for adult dogs or puppies, here are some helpful tips:

1. Always start on time. If the class is scheduled for 7:00 and only two out of seven dogs are present, start anyway. If you constantly wait for stragglers, people will know it's okay to arrive late. If you start on time, they will begin to show up on time, and even early; no one wants to miss out. It doesn't hurt, either, to randomly reward the first person to show up, or everyone who arrives promptly. A reward can be a piece of candy, coupons that can be collected and redeemed later for prizes, a clicker, or anything else you can think of.

2. Owners are often nervous the first day of class. Put them at ease by suggesting they not compare their dog's performance to others in the class. Dogs, like people, each learn at their own individual pace. The wonderful thing is that *their* dog will improve over the course of the class. It also helps to tell owners not to be embarrassed by barking or any other type of "misbehavior" their dog displays. After all, there would be no need for a class if all the dogs were already perfect!

3. While certain information is crucial to impart to your students, take care that your classes don't turn into lectures. If the subject is one that would take up a lot of class time, present it in a handout instead. People only process a small percentage of information given in lecture form anyway, so a handout is your best bet. Keep your classes moving along. Explain an exercise, demonstrate it with one of the student's dogs (don't pick the same one each time), then give feedback as the students practice. Alternate

exercises with games to keep things fresh and exciting. If you find people getting frustrated or tense during an exercise, take a quick break. Suggest that everyone stop, stretch and take a deep breath. This will put both people and dogs at ease and gives you time to think about how to break the exercise into smaller, easier pieces so everyone will succeed.

4. *Be as positive with the students as you are with the dogs.* This is extremely important! Some instructors are excellent with dogs, but have a way of making people feel badly. Rather than telling someone what they're doing is wrong, phrase it in a positive way, i.e. "That's a good start; now let's try this..." No one wants to be told they're doing something wrong, especially in front of a group. If you must point out something that is being done incorrectly, wait until the exercise is done, then address the class as a whole, i.e., "Here are some things to watch out for..." The only reason to single someone out in front of the group is to highlight something wonderful they or their dog have done. Remember, a good obedience class motivates both dogs and people and makes them feel good about themselves. It's fun, too, to give "rewards" to people for asking good questions or for doing something especially wonderful.

5. Structure your classes so exercises that require more energy, such as the Recall, are done at the beginning of class, while low-energy exercises such as Stay or Down are done toward the end, when the dogs are tired out. Smart structuring is one more way to set everyone up to succeed.

6. Keep instructions and concepts simple. Analogies are helpful for getting your point across. For example, when I talk about catching dogs doing something right and rewarding it, I often use this example: "Let's say every time you picked *that* chair to sit

in, I ran over and gave you a fifty dollar gift certificate. You can bet you'd be sitting in that chair more often! It's the same with your dog. If every time he lies calmly in his bed, you come over and give him a tummyrub, he'll be laying calmly in that bed a lot more often." Contrast that with saying, "Each time the dog presents the behavior, implement the conditioned reinforcer, followed by the reward." Uh-huh. See what I mean?

7. Remind owners to integrate what the dogs have learned into everyday situations. Once a dog learns Sit, the owner can have him sit before meals, going for walks, and anything else the dog finds rewarding. (This is also good for leadership.) Incorporate real-life games into your classes. For example, toward the end of a seven-week adult group session, we play a game which incorporates Leave It, Sit, Stay and Heel. I fill a paper grocery bag with empty egg cartons, plastic bottles and more, almost to the point of being overflowing. A course has been laid out which contains enticements the dogs must bypass, such as cookies on plates, a ball, etc. Each owner weaves through the course with their dog by their side on a loose leash, telling the dog to "Leave it" when necessary. At the end of the course is a doorway (which can be imaginary if you don't have a door nearby). The dog must sit and stay while the owner fumbles in their pocket for the key, puts the key in the door and opens it. The game is great fun and makes use of the skills dogs and owners have learned. Best of all, it's great practice for real-life situations.

8. Dogs don't generalize well. In other words, just because the dog understands what "Sit" means, it doesn't mean he will do it no matter what the conditions. For example, a lot of dogs learn that Sit means to sit facing their owner, with their owner standing in front of them. What often happens next, when the dog is expected to sit by the owner's side when the owner stops walking,

is that the dog's rear will swing out to the side. After all, Sit means to face the owner, right? It's important to "change the scene" for the dog. Sits should be practiced in different parts of the training area and in different positions such as facing the owner, by the owner's side, or with the owner sitting down. While it is important that owners practice at home with no distractions at first, encourage them to "take it on the road" by practicing in different rooms, in the back yard, front yard, sidewalk, and then in various locations away from home. Even having the owners take a different seat or position at each class is helpful.

9. Classes can be chaotic at times, especially if you're working with a large number of dogs. Teaching owners to reward their dog for paying attention will help immensely. If you are doing a clicker training class, have the owners click and treat any time the dog looks at them. Without clickers, have the owners say, "Yes!" each time the dog looks at them, then treat. Your classes will run much more smoothly and quietly if you can get owners to do this.

10. Point out to owners that one of the best tools they have for training their dogs is *their* behavior. Talk about how stress transfers down the leash, and how calm does as well. Rehearse with them what to do when their dog starts being reactive with another dog. Point out (nicely, of course!) when owners are starting to raise their voice, get tense, or otherwise influence the dog in a negative way with their own behavior.

11. Just as with in-home training, inevitably there will be people in your classes who are disruptive. Some will want to tell long, involved stories about their dog; some will ask more questions than you have time for; others will argue with just about anything you say. It's okay. Don't react. Those books in the *Resources*

section about dealing with people really are helpful. If someone is truly and repeatedly disruptive, speak with them privately after class or call them during the week and try to resolve the issues.

12. While it's great fun to be the center of attention and to hear comments about how wonderful you are, *it's not about you.* A good instructor is there to support students and their dogs, and to make *them* look good. After all, you're not the one the dogs will ultimately have to listen to. Students should think you're a good teacher, of course, but more importantly, they should come away feeling good about all they and their dog have learned, with a new confidence that *they* are good trainers.

Endnote

Hasta La Viszla, Baby!

Well, friend, this brings us to the end of our chat. I hope you have found the information in these pages helpful. Becoming a good trainer is a process, and this book is just the beginning. Take it a step at a time and try not to get overwhelmed. With experience will come confidence, knowledge and success. And remember, the best trainers are the ones who never stop learning!

Oh, one last thing... The time may come when you are a well-established trainer, and a novice trainer will contact you for help. Remember what it's like to be starting out and in need of assistance. Try not to see the other trainer as potential competition. There are certainly enough poorly behaved dogs to go around! Be generous and treat these trainers as you'd like others to have treated you at the beginning. The more positive trainers out there, the better.

Lots of luck, success and happy, wagging tails to you!

Resources

Recommended Books/Videos

There are many excellent books and videos available on training and behavior. While it would be impossible to list them all here, this collection should provide a great start to a well-rounded training education. Most are available through **Dogwise** at 1-800-776-2665 or www.dogwise.com, amazon.com or book stores.

Training & Behavior

Dog Language: An Encyclopedia of Canine Behavior
Roger Abrantes (Denmark)
Denmark: Wakan Tanka, Inc., 1997 ISBN 0-96604-840-7

Dog-Friendly Dog Training
Andrea Arden
New York, N.Y.: Howell Books, 1999 ISBN 1-582450099

Dogs Behaving Badly
Dr. Nicholas Dodman
New York, NY: Bantam Books ISBN 0-553-10873-5

The Culture Clash
Jean Donaldson
Oakland, CA: James & Kenneth Publishers, 1996 ISBN 1-888047-05-4

Dogs Are From Neptune
Jean Donaldson
Montreal, Quebec: Lasar Multimedia Productions Inc.,
1998 ISBN 0-9684207-1-0

So You Want To Be A Dog Trainer

Dog Behavior: An Owner's Guide to a Happy Healthy Pet
Ian Dunbar
IDG Books Worldwide, 1998 ISBN 0876052367

How to Teach a New Dog Old Tricks
Ian Dunbar
Oakland, CA: James & Kenneth Publishers, 1991 ISBN 1-888047-03-8

Sirius Puppy Training (video)
Ian Dunbar
Oakland, CA: James & Kenneth, 1987

Ian Dunbar's books and videos may be ordered directly from the publisher at James & Kenneth Publishers, 2140 Shattuck Avenue #2406, Berkeley, CA 94704   (510) 658-8588

The Cautious Canine (small, available in bulk, great handout)
(desensitization program for fearful/reactive dogs)
Patricia B. McConnell, Ph.D.
Black Earth, WI: Dog's Best Friend, Ltd., 1998 ISBN 1-891767-00-3

How to Be the Leader of The Pack
(small, available in bulk, great handout)
Patricia B. McConnell, Ph.D.
Black Earth, WI: Dog's Best Friend Ltd., 1996 ISBN 1-891767-02-X

I'll Be Home Soon (separation anxiety)
Patricia B. McConnell, Ph.D.
Black Earth, WI: Dog's Best Friend Ltd., 2000 ISBN 1-891767-05-4

The Power of Positive Dog Training
Pat Miller
New York: Hungry Minds, Inc., 2001 ISBN 0-7645-3609-5

Clinical Behavioral Medicine for Small Animals
(Textbook style, packed with valuable information. Includes extensive listing
of step-by-step protocols for modifying behavior problems.)
Karen L. Overall
St. Louis, Missouri: Mosby, 1997 ISBN 0-8016-6820-4

Taking Care of Puppy Business (small, available in bulk, great handout)
Gail Pivar and Leslie Nelson
Tails-U-Win, 1998
ph 1-847-741-2126
www.tailsuwin.com

Don't Shoot the Dog (includes some clicker training)
Karen Pryor
New York: Bantam Books, Inc., 1984 ISBN 0-553-25388-3

Excel-erated Learning
Pamela J. Reid, Ph.D.
Oakland, CA: James & Kenneth Publishers, 1996 ISBN 1888047070

The Instructor's Manual
John Rogerson
Wenatchee, WA: Direct Book Service, 1994

On Talking Terms with Dogs: Calming Signals
Turid Rugaas
Kula, HI: Legacy, 1997

The Bark Stops Here
Terry Ryan
Carlsborg, WA: Legacy By Mail, Inc., 2000 ISBN 0-9674796-2-2

The Toolbox for Remodeling Your Problem Dog
Terry Ryan
New York, NY: Simon & Schuster, 1998 ISBN 0-87605-049-6

So You Want To Be A Dog Trainer

Puppy Primer
Brenda K. Scidmore & Patricia B. McConnell, Ph.D.
Black Earth, WI: Dog's Best Friend, 1996 1-891767-01-1

Teaching Dog Obedience Classes
Joachim Volhard and Gail Fisher
New York, NY: Howell Book House: 1986 ISBN 0-87605-765-2

Clicker Training

Take A Bow Wow I & II
(videos on training tricks using clicker training)
Virginia Broitman & Sherry Lipman

Click and Go (video)
Click and Fix (video)
Dr. Deb Jones

*Teaching Clicker Classes: Instructor's Guide
to Using Reinforcement in Dog Training*
Deb Jones
Self-Published, 1996

Karen Pryor's Clicker Training Start-Up Kit (video/booklet/clicker)
Karen Pryor

Clicking with your Dog
Peggy Tillman
Waltham, MA: Sunshine Books, 2000 ISBN 1-890948-05-5

Click and Treat Training Kit (video/booklet/clicker)
Gary Wilkes

Breed Information

The Encyclopedia of the Dog
Bruce Fogle, D.V.M.
New York, NY: Dorling Kindersley, 1993 ISBN 0-7894-0149-5

Paws to Consider
Brian Kilcommons and Sarah Wilson
New York, NY: Warner Books, 1999 ISBN 0-446-52151-5

The Right Dog For You
Daniel F. Tortora, Ph.D.
New York, NY: Simon & Schuster, 1980 ISBN 0-671-47247-X

The Perfect Match: A Dog Buyer's Guide
Chris Walkowicz
New York, NY: Macmillan, 1996 ISBN 0-87605-767-9

Health, Nutrition, Natural Remedies

Give Your Dog A Bone (Raw foods diet)
Dr. Ian Billinghurst
N.S.W. Australia: Ian Billinghurst, 1993 ISBN 0-646-16028-1

The Natural Dog: A Complete Guide For Caring Owners
Mary L. Brennan, D.V.M.
New York, NY: Penguin Books, 1993 ISBN 0-452-27019-7

*The Healing Touch: The Proven Massage Program
for Cats and Dogs*
Michael W. Fox
Newmarket Press: 1990, ISBN 1557040621

Bach Flower Remedies for Animals
Helen Graham & Gregory Vlamis
Scotland: Findhorn Press, 1999 ISBN 1-899171-72-X

Dr. Pitcairn's Complete Guide to
Natural Health for Dogs & Cats
Pitcairn and Pitcairn
Emmaus, PA: Rodale Press, 1995 ISBN 0-87596-243-2

Natural Nutrition for Dogs and Cats (Raw foods diet)
Kymythy R. Schultze
Carlsbad, CA: Hay House, 1998 ISBN 1-56170-636-1

Natural Healing for Dogs & Cats
Diane Stein
Freedom, CA: The Crossing Press, Inc., 1993 ISBN 0-89594-686-6

Tellington TTouch Video/Workbook/
Flashcards/Manual For Dogs
Linda Tellington-Jones
Thane International, 1997

The Holistic Guide for a Healthy Dog
W. Volhard & D. Brown, DVM
New York, NY: MACMILLAN, 1995 ISBN 0-87605-560-9

Counseling People

Dog Behavior Problems: The Counselor's Handbook
William E. Campbell
Behaviorx Systems 1999, ISBN 0966870514

The Evans Guide for Counseling Dog Owners
Job Michael Evans
New York, NY: Howell Book House, Inc., 1985 ISBN 0-87605-660-5

(Also, go to www.amazon.com and do a search with "difficult people" as the subject.)

Miscellaneous Books

Fun and Games with Dogs
Roy Hunter
United Kingdom: Howlin' Moon Press, 1995 ISBN 1888994002

Games People Play To Train Their Dogs (great game ideas for classes) and *Life Beyond Block Heeling* (volume two of the above)
Terry Ryan
WA: Legacy By Mail, 1996

Coercion and its Fallout
(Effects of the use of force on people and animals)
Murray Sidman
Boston, MA: Authors Cooperative, Inc., 1989 ISBN 0962331112

How To Market Your Dog Training Business
Lisa K. Wilson
CA: The Dog Trainers Marketing Resource Center, 1997

Clickers, Target Sticks, Bait Bags & More

www.dogwise.com
www.legacybymail.com
www.sitstay.com

Other Publications

The Clicker Journal
Victoria Farrington
4040 Rosewell Plantation Rd.
Gloucester, CA 23061
www.clickertrain.com/journal.html

Pet Behavior Newsletter
P.O. Box 1658
Grants Pass, OR 97526
www.webtrail.com/petbehavior/index.html

Sue Sternberg's booklets and videos
(Great info on temperament testing, defensive handling,
food aggression and more)
Rondout Valley Kennels
4628 Route 209
Accord, NY 12404
914-687-4406
www.suesternberg.com

The Whole Dog Journal
P.O. Box 420234
Palm Coast, FL 32142
Subscriptions 1-800-829-9165
Back issues 1-800-424-7887

Organizations & Education

ABTA (Animal Behavior and Training Associates)
(ABTA teaches all PetCo classes)
1-800-795-3294

Association of Pet Dog Trainers (APDT)
66 Morris Avenue #2A
Springfield, N.J. 07081
1-800-PET-DOGS
www.apdt.com

Moorpark College
7075 Campus Road
Moorpark, CA 93021
805-378-1400
www.moorpark.cc.ca.us

PETsMART Pet Training Program
1-800-738-1385

San Fransisco SPCA Academy For Dog Trainers
(415) 554-3095
www.sfspca.org/behavior%20&training/academy/
bt_academy.html

Products

Assess-A-Hand
Rondout Valley Kennels
4628 Route 209
Accord, NY 12404
845-687-7619
www.suesternberg.com

Bark Bars
American Health Kennels
4351 N.E. 11th Ave.
Pompano Beach, FL 33064
954-781-0730

Gentle Leaders, Premier Collars and more
Premier Pet Products
406 Branchway Rd.
Richmond, VA 23236
1-800-933-5595

KISS Manufacturing
Promotional products including fridge magnets
1-800-262-2868
www.kissmfg.com

Kong Company
303-216-2626
www.kongcompany.com

My Dog Can Do That!
Board game, great for graduation class
Available through Dogwise

Online Information

An Animal Trainer's Introduction to
Classical and Operant Conditioning
Stacy Braslau-Schneck's articles on the above.
www.geocities.com/Athens/Academy/8636/Clicker.html

Clicker Solutions Training Treasures
A collection of articles/posts on clicker training,
solving behavior problems and more from the Clicker
Solutions internet list. (See *Internet Lists*)
Training Treasures (posts from list):
www.clickersolutions.com/clickersolutions/treasures/
treasurecontents.htm
Articles: www.clickersolutions.com/clickersolutions/articles/
articlecontents.htm

Dog Owner's Guide
Articles on training, breed profiles, and more.
www.canismajor.com

Dr. P's Dog Training
A collection of free online articles about training,
learning theory and more by Dr. Mark Plonsky, Ph.D.
www.uwsp.edu/psych/dog/dog.htm

Flying Dog Press
Free, online articles by Suzanne Clothier on dog
training and behavior.
www.flyingdogpress.com

Lasardogs
Jean Donaldson's Dogs Behaving Badly site
Video clips of Kong stuffing, training articles and more.
www.lasardogs.com

Puppyworks
Information on upcoming educational dog events.
www.puppyworks.com

Rec.pets.dogs FAQ
Frequently Asked Questions from the Usenet group
Rec.pets.dogs, answered by Cindy Tittle Moore -
includes collection of training articles.
www.k9web.com/dog-faqs

The Well Mannered Dog
Shirley Chong's Keeper Pages - a collection of
training articles and posts from internet groups,
focusing on clicker training.
www.shirleychong.com/keepers/index.html

Internet Lists

There are countless mailing lists concerning dog behavior and
training on the internet. These are just a few:

Agbeh (Aggression Behaviors in Dogs)
http://groups.yahoo.com/agbeh

APDT-L (open to APDT members only)
http://groups.yahoo.com/group/apdtlist

Clicker Solutions
www.clickersolutions.com/clickersolutions/cshome.htm

Click-L
www.click-l.com

ClickTeach (for clicker training instructors)
http://groups.yahoo.com/clickteach

ClickTrain
http://groups.yahoo.com/group/clicktrain

Shelter Trainers List
http://groups.yahoo.com/group/sheltertrainers

Miscellaneous

Liability Insurance For Dog Trainers:

Business Insurers
(Offers insurance specifically to APDT members)
1-800-962-4611

The Hartford Insurance Co.
1-888-253-4940